the reflective early years
Practitioner

Education at SAGE

SAGE is a leading international publisher of journals, books, and electronic media for academic, educational, and professional markets.

Our education publishing includes:

- accessible and comprehensive texts for aspiring education professionals and practitioners looking to further their careers through continuing professional development

- inspirational advice and guidance for the classroom

- authoritative state of the art reference from the leading authors in the field

Find out more at: **www.sagepub.co.uk/education**

the reflective early years
Practitioner

elaine hallet

Los Angeles | London | New Delhi
Singapore | Washington DC

Los Angeles | London | New Delhi
Singapore | Washington DC

SAGE Publications Ltd
1 Oliver's Yard
55 City Road
London EC1Y 1SP

SAGE Publications Inc.
2455 Teller Road
Thousand Oaks, California 91320

SAGE Publications India Pvt Ltd
B 1/I 1 Mohan Cooperative Industrial Area
Mathura Road
New Delhi 110 044

SAGE Publications Asia-Pacific Pte Ltd
3 Church Street
#10-04 Samsung Hub
Singapore 049483

Editor: Jude Bowen
Editorial assistant: Miriam Davey
Production editor: Jeanette Graham
Assisant production editor: Nicola Marshall
Copyeditor: Carol Lucas
Proofreader: Isabel Kirkwood
Marketing manager: Lorna Patkai
Cover design: Wendy Scott
Typeset by: C&M Digitals (P) Ltd, Chennai, India
Printed in India at Replika Press Pvt Ltd

Library of Congress Control Number: 2012934591

British Library Cataloguing in Publication data

A catalogue record for this book is available from
the British Library

ISBN 978-1-4462-0055-1
ISBN 978-1-4462-0056-8 (pbk)

I dedicate this book to all early years practitioners who work with young children and their families.

Contents

List of Figures

About the Author

Dr Elaine Hallet is Lecturer in Early Childhood Education at the Institute of Education: University of London, England. She teaches on undergraduate and postgraduate courses and supervises research students. She has wide experience of working with practitioners, children and families as a teacher, advisory teacher and deputy head teacher; in further and higher education as a lecturer, departmental leader and researcher. Her research interests include children's early literacy learning, curriculum and leadership in the early years. Elaine's doctorate focused on early years practitioners' continuous professional learning in higher education. She contributes regularly to professional and academic publications, and presents at national and international conferences.

Acknowledgements

I would like to thank and acknowledge the contribution of many who have provided reflective insights and encouragement in the development and writing of this book. Thanks to Jude Bowen and Miriam Davey at SAGE for enabling my authorship and guidance in completing the book; the peer-reviewers for their time and valuable feedback; my friends and family for their support and patience; and my parents for belief in education. Also, thanks to the colleagues I have worked with over the years, the times we have reflected and learnt together, and the practitioners and students I have learnt from in the various colleges and universities in which I have taught; the students who gave me feedback on reflective activities used in class; and the practitioners who gave permission to use examples of their practice as case studies.

Finally, a special thank you, to all the women graduates in the research study who went on this learning journey of reflective discovery and understanding with me, their time and reflections made them true travelling companions.

Glossary of Terms

ADCE	Advanced Diploma in Childcare and Education
APcL	Accredited Prior credit Learning
APEL	Accredited Prior Experimental Learning
BA	Bachelor of Arts undergraduate degree
BA(Hons)	Bachelor of Arts undergraduate degree with honours
CCSK	Common Core of Skills and Knowledge
CPD	Continuing Professional Development
CWDC	Children's Workforce Development Council
DCSF	Department for Children Schools and Families
DES	Department for Education and Science
DfE	Department for Education
DfEE	Department for Education and Employment
DfES	Department for Education and Skills
EAZ	Education Action Zone
ECEC	Early Childhood Education and Care
EPPE	The Effective Provision of Pre-school Education Project
ELEYS	The Effective Leadership in the Early Years Sector Study
EYFS	Early Years Foundation Stage
EYP	Early Years Professional
EYPS	Early Years Professional Status
EYSEFD	Early Years Sector-Endorsed Foundation Degree
FD	Foundation Degree
FDF	Foundation Degree Forward
FE	Further education
GTTP	Graduate Teacher Training Programme
HE	Higher education
HLTA	Higher Level Teaching Assistant
IEP	Individual Education Plan
MA	Master's degree
NPQICL	National Professional Qualification for Integrated Centre Leadership
NVQ	National Vocational Qualification
Ofsted	Office for Standards in Education
PVI	Private, voluntary and independent sector
QAA	Quality Assurance Agency
QCF	Qualifications and Credit Framework
QTS	Qualified Teacher Status

SCIT	School Centred Initial Training
SEN	Special educational needs
SENCO	Special Educational Needs Co-ordinator
SEYFD	Sector-Endorsed Early Years Foundation Degree
SPS	Senior Practitioner Status
TA	Teaching Assistant
TDA	Teaching Development Agency
UNCRN	United Nations Convention on the Rights of the Child

Introduction

As the title implies, this book is about early years practitioners who are reflective. The title, *The Reflective Early Years Practitioner,* refers to the centrality of reflection for practitioners working in the early years sector with children, families and multi-professionals in early years settings, schools, children's centres, in integrated practice and children's services. Reflection in its broadest sense is threaded throughout the book, craftily stitched within and across the pages, and woven around the concept of *a reflective early years practitioner* in layers of textured, shiny and shimmering threads illuminating the qualities, attributes and behaviours of reflective early years practitioners.

The journey of becoming and being a *reflective early years practitioner* is storied throughout the chapters in a developmental way, reflecting the evolving roles and responsibilities of the early years workforce; emerging from an 'invisible' workforce of nursery nurses quietly washing paint pots in the corner of an infant classroom, to a 'visible' workforce of leaders with agency who are in the frontline of shaping and leading provision and practice.

The majority of the early years workforce are women. Their journeying through the pages celebrates their progression and achievement through continuing professional learning, vocational and academic achievement in higher education, and progression through employment opportunities into a unique and specialized workforce. While the author recognizes the role of men within the early years workforce and does not wish to exclude them, this book focuses upon women practitioners within the early years workforce. It unravels and understands women's personal and professional challenges and opportunities, and their transformation through reflective learning within the work context and higher education.

The term 'early years practitioner' used throughout the book is a generic term inclusive of gender, ethnicity, age, ability and disability, referring to adults who work with young children and families in the broadest sense as educators, teachers, health and social care workers, in settings, schools, children's centres, children's services and home-based provision.

Reflection within a landscape of change

Reflection is a key attribute to being a 'reflective early years practitioner', the development of a reflective early years workforce is important for thoughtful and considered implementation of policy into practice, particularly within the current changing and evolving early years landscape of government review and policy. Workforce reform in the Children's Workforce Strategy (DfES, 2005) further developed a graduate-led sector to raise the quality of provision in the non-maintained sector through undergraduate and foundation degrees, and professional awards such as Early Years Sector-Endorsed Foundation Degrees (EYSEFDs) and Early Years Professional Status (EYPS) graduate leadership programmes. In these awards there are opportunities for practitioners and students to reflect upon their practice. Reflection provides agency for practitioners to lead, shape and develop provision and practice in settings, schools, children's centres, integrated children's services and home-based provision. The ability for practitioners to reflect is important in developing a reflective early years workforce. Evidence from the longitudinal study of graduate leader training suggests that graduate leaders' ability to reflect is improving provision and practice in early years settings and children's centres (Hadfield et al., 2011).

The work of Donald Schon (1987) introduced the notion of 'the reflective practitioner', a practitioner who engages in reflective practice. There has been a tradition of teachers using reflection to consider their professional practice, and modify and develop teaching approaches in nursery and primary schools (McGregor and Cartwright, 2011). Reflective practice is a relatively new concept to practitioners working in the early years sector in settings other than schools, such as private day nurseries, play groups, children's centres, full and sessional care, and home-based providers such as childminders. There is an emerging body of writing about reflective practice in the early years, for example by Paige-Smith and Craft (2011) and Reed and Canning (2010). The introduction of foundation degrees in 2000 introduced higher educational pedagogy for vocational learning. In 2001, the introduction of EYSEFD as a work-based learning award provided a long awaited professional learning opportunity for experienced practitioners working in the early years sector. Rawlings (2008) has written about studying work-based learning in the early years. However, the concepts of reflective practice and work-based learning are written about separately. This book draws the two ideas together, in the concept of work-based reflective learning.

Through a research study of an EYSEFD, the relationship between work-based learning and reflective practice was identified as key to the development of reflective practitioners; reflective practice is developed through work-based reflective learning. Work-based reflective learning enables a practitioner to become a reflective early years practitioner or to further develop reflective behaviour as a reflective early years practitioner. Work-based reflective learning is a transformational agency for change and development in provision and practice, and practitioners' professional learning and development. The concept of work-based reflective learning is discussed throughout the book and illustrated in a model of work-based reflective learning in Chapter 3.

The research context

The Reflective Early Years Practitioner discusses the author's doctoral research completed in 2008. A case study of an EYSEFD delivered in a collaborative further education/higher education (FE/HE) partnership based in the Midlands region formed her doctoral thesis. The programme was delivered at the lead university, in three further education colleges and two outreach centres in four different local authorities. The graduates were one of the first cohorts nationally to be awarded the sector-endorsed foundation degree (EYSEFD) with Senior Practitioner Status (SPS) and the first cohort of graduates to be awarded a foundation degree (FD) at the lead university.

The programme ran for five years and was a large part of my professional life. I was seconded from a further education college to become part of the Development Team in developing, writing and validating the programme. On the day of validation we were invited to apply for the programme to be sector endorsed. After writing the application the FD programme was endorsed as a Department for Education (DfE) SureStart Recognized foundation degree and the university was recognized as a provider. For the FD to be nationally recognized and sector endorsed, the higher education provider had to demonstrate that the curriculum and their institution as a provider met nationally required criteria. Along with this recognition came a financial support package for students, including payment of fees and childcare costs, bursaries for books, supply cover to attend college or university and a laptop personal computer for study. This support package opened opportunity and access to higher education for many students, particularly women, and recruitment was high. As Programme Leader, I taught on the programme and led the tutor team for five enjoyable years. For the first FD graduates, I helped design the hood for the graduates to wear over their gown; to see them walk across the stage in their cap and gown at graduation was a memorable sight.

The research study arose out of a Quality Assurance Agency (QAA) Review of the EYSEFD; a graduate commented to one of the reviewers

'This Foundation Degree was life changing, I wouldn't have got my job without it'. How had the FD programme contributed to vocational employment progression of this graduate? Her comment made me reflect; what were the significant components of the programme? How had the FD programme developed the graduates professionally? This was the starting point for the research. Two research aims developed:

- To examine the foundation degree as a vocational higher education award.
- To examine the impact of the foundation degree upon early years practitioners' vocational progression, personal and professional development.

Although the research examines a foundation degree, the key findings and discussion within the chapters is relevant to other undergraduate and postgraduate higher education programmes, raising relevant issues for the developing workforce of early years leaders and professional practitioners.

The research sample group comprised of 65 women FD graduates who studied in part-time evening provision. They were employed as support staff in roles as nursery nurses, teaching assistants and nursery managers, in a range of early years settings and schools, and within integrated children's services. The sample had representatives from all delivery sites; all participants were women, representative of the predominantly female workforce.

The research study had four different phases of data collection:

- Phase One –   Documentation
- Phase Two –   Questionnaires
- Phase Three – Narrative Qualitative Interviews
- Phase Four –   Reflective Learning Journeys.

A feminist paradigm and methodological approach empathetic to the sample group of women practitioners underpinned the research, data collection methods, analysis and discussion of findings. The Emergent Method Approach (Nagy Hesse-Biber and Leavy, 2006) developed an emergent and reflective cycle of data collection; the data findings collected in each phase informed the next phase of data collection. This reflective cycle of emergent research is sympathetic with the grounded-theory method of simultaneous data collection and analysis, with each informing and focusing the other throughout the research process. The constructivist approach to data collection created theory grounded in the actual experience and language of women (Kitzinger, 2007). Olesen (2005: 236) defines feminist qualitative research as 'highly diversified, enormously dynamic and thoroughly challenging, using a variety of qualitative modes using both experimental and text orientated styles'. This approach was used in Phase Four in the data collection process in Reflective Learning Journeys, in which pictorial and narrative representation are used in an experimental way to record women's autobiographical experiences. Feminist qualitative research focuses upon women's standpoints and their everyday world, one that is continually created, shaped and known by women within it in a biographical way. To understand this world, the researcher must work alongside women, and co-construct meaning in a reflective way (Smith, 1992) so the 'view from nowhere becomes the view from somewhere' (Haraway, 1988: 251). The research methods aimed to empower the participants and allow them to contribute to determining the most prominent themes (Elliott, 2006). The use of autobiographical verbal, visual and written narrative in interviewing and recording the women's learning journeys allowed for individual 'women's voices to be heard and listened to' about what they had to say about their experience (Kitzinger, 2007: 113). A biographical approach to research gets inside each participant, highlighting their perspective. Narrative has the potential to develop identity formation over time (Seale et al., 2007: 48) and is like fingerprints, individually unique marks, as the women's Reflective Learning Journeys in Chapter 9 illustrate.

Organization of the book

Work-based reflective learning is a thread woven throughout the book, enabling the reader to develop their own reflective thinking, behaviour and professional practice through each chapter. A range of *case studies* from early years settings, schools, children's centres and children's services provide a rich tapestry of examples of practice, stitching practice with theory. *Questions for reflection* provide a framework for reflective thinking and learning. A range of *figures* illustrate aspects of work-based reflective learning and pedagogy. The book aims to be a resource for reflection for practitioners and students to develop their professional learning and practice as reflective early years practitioners.

Each chapter is based upon research findings from my doctoral research study about women graduates' experiences of an EYSEFD pro-gramme, referred to as 'the FD case study' throughout the book. The chapters are also informed by my work as a lecturer in higher edu-cation in enabling undergraduate and postgraduate students in their

continuous professional reflective learning. At the end of their FD studies, the graduates, through work-based reflective learning, emerged
as reflective early years practitioners, a transformed workforce with
agency and a professional identity, a unique female workforce in the
frontline of leading settings, children's centres and children's services,
turning government policy into practice. Their authentic voices are
heard throughout the chapters as *practitioners' reflective voices*, women
graduates reflecting upon their continuing vocational and academic
professional learning, their work with children, families and multi-
professionals. In the last two chapters, women graduates reflect upon
their vocational and academic learning journey through higher
education and their continuing professional learning pathways. Their
real-life narratives provide insights into their personal and professional
learning and development, illuminating the transformational and
empowering agency of work-based reflective learning.

The chapter contents story practitioners' higher educational journey
as a reflective early years workforce. Each chapter builds upon the one
before, but can also be read individually as a themed chapter. The
following provides a summary of each chapter.

Chapter 1, 'The developing early years practitioner', explores
the development of the early years workforce through broadening
of roles and responsibilities, continuing professional learning and
employment opportunities. The emergence of early years practitioners working in supportive roles to a confident workforce of leaders
and managers with active agency is storied through the chapter.
There is opportunity to reflect upon your work-based progression, as
a developing early years practitioner.

Chapter 2, 'Being a reflective early years practitioner', discusses
how engaging in reflective learning within the work context has enabled
early years practitioners to become reflective practitioners working
professionally with young children, families and other professionals.
There is opportunity to discuss theories of reflection and to reflect
upon your own work-based reflective learning throughout the chapter.

Chapter 3, 'Work-based reflective learning', examines work-based
reflective learning as a process for reflective change in provision and
practice. The relationship with work-based learning and reflection is
illustrated in a model of 'work-based reflective learning', demonstrating the process of reflective learning within the work context of professional practice. There is opportunity to use the model of work-based
reflective learning to reflect upon practice.

Chapter 4, 'Reflective vocational progression', further explores
work-based reflective learning. Its contribution to practitioners'

professional progression, employment opportunities and vocational work with children and families is explored through five themes: professional vocational practice; academic and professional knowledge; enhanced employability; lifelong learning and progression; and work-based research and practice. The themes are illuminated by reflective practitioners' voices and case studies. There is opportunity to reflect upon your vocational progression.

Chapter 5, 'Work-based reflective pedagogy', discusses work-based reflective learning as pedagogy for vocational continuing professional development in higher education. The concept of 'wrap-around-learning' provides a model for flexible study and access to higher education. Reflective practitioners' voices and a case study provide examples of professional learning through work-based reflective pedagogy. You are able to consider your continuous professional learning through reflective questions.

Chapter 6, 'Being a reflective student', provides students with study skills for reflective study and becoming independent reflective learners, acknowledging the learning environment, community of learners and practice each student joins and contributes to, within their work setting and the higher education environment in which they study. The chapter guides the student to become a reflective student, providing practical help for reflective learning and study through reflective activities.

Chapter 7, 'Reflecting upon professionalism in the early years', explores the evolving professional landscape in the early years, reflecting upon professionalization and practitioners' emerging professional identity within the early years sector through higher education and graduate leadership training in reflective discussion. There is opportunity to reflect upon your developing professional identity.

Chapter 8, 'Reflective leadership', builds upon the previous chapter by examining specific leadership characteristics and style, practices and behaviours of early years leaders within the context of a developing graduate-led early years sector. The reflective thinking and learning skills required for leading within, across and beyond early years settings, schools, children's centres and children's services as a reflective leader are explored.

Chapter 9, 'Reflective learning journeys', considers the theme of reflective learning through examples of women graduate practitioners' reflective learning journeys through their higher education experiences. Key influences upon the graduates' academic, vocational and career progression are identified. The women's reflective voices about their individual and unique learning journeys aim to inspire students and early years practitioners to begin, or continue, their journey into learning.

Chapter 10, 'Continuing learning pathways and future reflections', discusses practitioners' continuing learning pathways in the current early years landscape of reform and change. The contribution of early years practitioners' professional knowledge and research in influencing others and implementing change in provision and practice is examined through case studies. The role of reflective early years practitioners in encouraging children to engage in reflection is also explored.

Further reading is suggested at the end of each chapter as an opportunity to extend understanding of key themes and concepts discussed in the chapter to enhance and further knowledge. There is an extensive reference list at the back of the book to further signpost reading.

Concluding reflections

Finally, this introduction has been the last part of the book written, and provided a reflective space for me to once again think about the purpose of the book and who the readers may be. You may be an undergraduate or postgraduate student, an early years practitioner, children's centre manager, a teacher or a lecturer. Whoever you are, I hope the contents of the book will illuminate new ideas and knowledge about reflective learning and provide a source for reflective questioning, thinking and conversations with others while you work and study.

I have been on two professional *reflective learning journeys*, the first during the research study, the second during the writing of this book. Both were at times smooth and bumpy, experiencing challenges and opportunities along the way. At the final destination of each journey, I had learnt a lot and developed professionally. I now invite you to embark on your own reflective learning journey through the pages of the book.

With suitcases packed, tickets and passports in hand, let the journey begin . . .

1

The Developing Early Years Practitioner

Chapter overview

For many years, adults working with babies and young children undertook a caring role. The roles and responsibilities of early years practitioners have broadened across education, health and social services. Professional learning and employment opportunities have enabled the development of a knowledgably confident workforce. The revealing of early years practitioners to a visible workforce with active agency is storied through the chapter. There is opportunity to reflect upon your work-based progression as a developing early years practitioner.

This chapter will:
- Explore the development of early years practitioners' roles and responsibilities.
- Examine historical, research influences and government policy upon workforce reform.
- Discuss the gender construct of the early years workforce.
- Consider the contribution of practitioners' professional learning upon setting, school and service provision.
- Consider the development of a graduate-led workforce.

Developing roles and responsibilities

Traditionally, nursery nurses were the main practitioners working with babies and young children. Their role has developed with more responsibilities as they have furthered their engagement with children, families and multi-professionals in a range of early years contexts and integrated services. If you were able to go back in time to a nursery or infant classroom 30 years ago, nursery nurses working there would be quietly washing paint pots and brushes in the sink in the corner of the infant classroom or nursery – one of the many daily routine tasks nursery nurses carried out. These routine tasks also included sharpening pencils, cutting paper, tidying the book corner, washing dirty clothes; all low-graded tasks that, in many cases, the nursery or school teacher preferred not to undertake. However, these were important tasks supporting the work of the teacher, allowing the teacher more time for teaching children. The teacher's higher qualification and skills as a qualified graduate teacher enabled her or him to teach the class or group of nursery children, which a less qualified nursery nurse was unable to do. Nursery nurses worked under the direction of a teacher with small groups of children. It depended upon the nursery or school they worked in how involved they were in planning activities and attending staff meetings. Some nursery nurses participated in planning meetings and attended staff meetings; some were not allowed in the staffroom. Nursery nurses were considered as non-teaching support staff; the exclusion zones reinforced this view.

In the twenty-first century, nursery nurses are no longer an invisible workforce who are 'just washing the paint pots'. They are a visible workforce working with babies, young children, practitioners, professionals and agencies in leadership and management roles, and in complementary teaching roles, undertaking diverse roles within integrated practice in a range of services for children and families, in schools and early years settings, children's centres and integrated children's services in both the maintained and private, voluntary and independent (PVI) sectors. The invisible workforce has been transformed into a visible workforce through professional learning and new employment opportunities.

The job titles for practitioners other than teachers, working in the early years are varied, at times confusing and often not reflecting the diversity of the role undertaken. Job titles reflect the value of that role to parents and to others. The terminology used around a job can cause misconceptions about the role and responsibilities within it (Adams, 2008). The following array of job titles is used for practitioners and teachers working with young children in nurseries and early years settings, children's centres, schools and home-based provision (Hallet, 2008b):

- Childminder
- Children's Centre Teacher
- Classroom Assistant
- Crèche Worker
- Early Years Educator
- Early Years Practitioner
- Early Years Professional
- Early Years Teacher

- Foundation Stage Co-ordinator
- High Level Teaching Assistant
- Learning Support Assistant
- Learning Mentor
- Nanny
- Nursery Nurse
- Nursery Assistant
- Nursery Manager
- Nursery Teacher
- Play Leader
- Pre-school Leader
- Room Leader
- Room Supervisor
- Senior Nursery Nurse
- Teaching Assistant.

The variety of names for various job roles reflects how one suitable title has not been found to describe the complexity of the work of the early years workforce. The term 'nursery nurse' is still the common generic term for those working with young children other than teachers (Adams, 2008), while the term 'teaching assistant' (TA) has become the common generic term for support staff working in schools, acknowledging their contribution to teaching and learning and pupil achievement (DfEE, 2000). The development of integrated practice highlights the case for a new language referring to those working in children's services, with emphasis on an integrated pedagogical approach to working practices (Cameron, 2004).

In the care and education of young children there has been a long history of including the word 'nursery' in a job title, for example, nursery nurse, nursery assistant and nursery manager, to describe the work of early years practitioners other than teachers. The names derive from the qualification and job role of a nursery nurse, a term from Victorian times, when women worked in children's nurseries as nurses looking after the physical health of children in their care. The emphasis on children's health and well-being was promoted by the McMillan sisters (1860–1931). In their open-air nursery schools, children played out on large verandas to breathe in the fresh air associated with robust health – a contrast to the foggy air in the slums of London (MacLeod-Brudenell, 2008). The job title of 'nursery nurse' described this health carer's role well, before education became part of nursery provision (Hallet, 2008b) and continues to be used. Whenever the term 'nursery nurse' is used, it misrepresents the valuable and complex role of caring and educating young children, and working with parents, carers and families. Many qualified nursery nurses undertake management and leadership roles, using a range of knowledge and skills developed through experience of working in early years provision, as the following case study shows.

📁 **Case study:** *A morning in the life of a nursery nurse*

Edee qualified as a nursery nurse 10 years ago, she works in a large private day nursery. Her working day begins early in the morning, ending late in the evening. Her day begins earlier at home: she gets up her own children, washes, dresses and gives them breakfast, gets them into the car, dropping them off at the childminder's before arriving at the nursery for her working day to begin.

She is the Deputy Manager but today she is Acting Manager as her manager is out for the day on a course. She is able to sit in her chair and even answer the phone . . . But responsibility goes with that. She looks in the diary and there are meetings with parents and a staff meeting to organize. Edee usually works in the Toddler Room; she goes there to brief the supply nursery nurse, covering her role for the day, introducing the parents to her replacement.

Her first meeting is with a prospective new parent who wishes to use the nursery for her baby as she returns to work from maternity leave. Edee greets the parent and her 1-year-old baby and, after introductions and giving the parent the nursery's prospectus, she takes her on a tour of the setting, introducing staff, and explaining the curriculum and provision. On return to her office, she answers the parent's queries and offers the parent a place for her baby in the nursery, beginning the following week.

Her next meeting is with the nursery's cook and a parent who has complained about the quality of the food her child had received, while attending nursery. The parent explained her child, Zoe, wouldn't eat the food provided; she was concerned about the little amount of food she was eating during her time at nursery. The cook explained about the nursery's healthy eating menu, defending her cooking and the quality of the ingredients she used. Edee acted as a mediator between the cook and the parent during a lengthy discussion. Edee helped a compromise to be reached; the parent providing some of Zoe's lunch, the cook providing some food Zoe liked. Both left the meeting happier than when they arrived.

There is a staff meeting to plan with a focus on developing the outside as a learning area. Edee had recently been on a course, 'Taking the inside outside', so prepared a small PowerPoint presentation about the benefits of learning outdoors. She made an agenda for the meeting, including time for the staff to contribute ideas and about how the nursery's outdoor area could be developed for learning. Edee wanted staff to develop ideas and produce a development plan for this initiative to progress by the end of the meeting, so it was important to have a focused agenda with ample time for this thinking to take place. She then joined the staff in the staffroom for her sandwich lunch.

The following questions will enable you to reflect upon Edee's role. She used a range of knowledge and skills as the Acting Nursery Manager in the meetings with the new parent, the cook and the parent, and in planning the staff meeting.

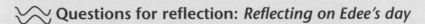

Questions for reflection: *Reflecting on Edee's day*

Can you identify when she used the following knowledge and skills during these meetings and activity?

- Effective communication
- Marketing
- Decision-making
- Conflict resolution
- Negotiation
- Planning
- Knowledge transfer
- Collaboration.

Following from this reflection, consider the term 'nursery nurse'.

- Does the term 'nursery nurse' really describe Edee's complex and varied role?
- Is there a term that would describe her job role more fully?

The term 'nursery nurse' promotes the gendered nature of the early years workforce which is now considered.

A female workforce

Traditionally, the early years sector has a predominantly female workforce (Kay, 2005), cultural and social conditioning being responsible for establishing female and male gender roles. Patriarchal systems of society maintain caring for children is naturally women's work (Roberts-Holmes and Brownhill, 2011). Women as child bearers undertake a mothering and nurturing role in the care of children. Many young girls have responded to their career teacher's question 'What do you want to do when you leave school?' with the reply, 'I want to work with children' and have been directed to the local further education college to attend a childcare course.

Females being associated with children are socially constructed through the mothering role, traditionally carried out by women. Women interacting with babies and children in a patient, caring and nurturing way are viewed as having qualities associated with motherhood, therefore in working with children, women will meet babies' and children's needs in a caring way (Reynolds, 1996). There is an assumption that caring for young children is an easy job that can be done by anyone who is kind, loving, warm and sensitive, and who likes children. McGillvray (2008) refers to this as the 'Mary Poppins syndrome'. Browne (2008) describes 'feminine traits' of emotions, sensitivity, creativity and care as integral to working in the early years sector. Through gendered perceptions and the socialization of girls and women, working with babies and young children as nursery nurses, teaching assistants, home-based nannies and childminders, seems attractive, therefore producing a predominantly female workforce.

The gender construct that working with children is women's work, something that women do naturally and are intrinsically better at (Moss, 2003; Peeters, 2007) has influenced the value of the work as of low status. Workforce reform and the development of a graduate-led workforce in the Children's Workforce Strategy (DfES, 2005) is raising the status of the early years workforce but without the reward of increased level of pay. Early years services are critical for the development of young children. However, the workforce is one of the lowest paid and the least qualified (Cooke and Lawton, 2008). Gender is inextricably part of the workforce (McGillivray, 2008); gender role association, low status, low pay and the high proportion of females in the workforce interact with one another (Cooke and Lawton, 2008). Practitioners working in the early years, who are not qualified as teachers, are seen with less regard, which is reflected in low pay (Kay 2005). Historically, the early years workforce is 'under qualified, underpaid and overwhelmingly female' (Miller and Cable, 2008b: 120), a challenge which is beginning to be addressed through government funded higher education and professional awards in raising qualifications, status and professional confidence of the early years workforce (Hadfield et al., 2011).

A smaller number of male practitioners and teachers work with young children mainly in schools, but also in early years settings, children's centres, children's services, and in the extended schools service. Although the numbers of men employed in the early years sector is increasing, male workers are regarded as exceptions to the general rule that childcare is work for women (Cameron et al., 1999). Early childcare and education as gendered women's work, assumes a female workforce reproducing its own patterns of recruitment and training. An examination of gender pedagogy may increase recruitment of men (Peeters, 2007).

Gender is threaded throughout interactions with parents and professionals and within practitioners' everyday professional practice,
whether the practitioner or teacher is female or male. In the development of a more highly qualified workforce, generic characteristics for
those working within children's services are important, rather than
focusing upon gender differences. There is an assumption that children need male practitioners and teachers as role models in their educational experiences. Research by Carrington et al. (2007) found the
gender of the practitioner had little influence upon children's level of
educational achievement. Practitioners' pedagogical and interpersonal
skills are more important in engaging children in learning (Roberts-
Holmes and Brownhill, 2011).

The predominantly female workforce with feminine characteristics,
traits and qualities should be celebrated; they are leaders of professional
practice in an evolving landscape of government policy. Through
access to continuing professional learning, professional knowledge and
confidence, a workforce with active agency has developed.

Developing quality through professional awards

Two significant pieces of research, the Rumbold Report (DES, 1990) and
the Effective Provision of Pre-School Education Project (EPPE Project)
(Sylva et al., 2010), bridge a decade in time but both demonstrate the
link between quality of provision and the quality of the workforce,
having implications for training and continuing professional development (CPD). The Tickell Review of the Early Years Foundation
Stage (EYFS) curriculum highlights the importance of an experienced,
strong, well-qualified and supported workforce upon the educational outcomes of children (Tickell, 2011). The Foundation Years Qualifications
Review (Nutbrown, 2012) reviews existing qualifications within the
government's review of provision in 2010–2012. A key issue within
the review is the content and delivery of early years training courses,
highlighting that learning should take place through an integrated
balance of high-quality practical experience, theory-based learning
and critical reflection.

Historically, the Rumbold Report (DES, 1990) was a catalyst for change
in reforming the early years workforce. The report found inequality of
educational provision for 3- and 4-year-olds, highlighting the need
for a high-quality experience for children, recognizing working with
young children is 'a demanding and complex task, those working
in it need a range of attributes to ensure high quality experience for
children' (DES, 1990: 19). The report identified ways to improve quality

of service by raising the qualifications of the workforce through staff development opportunities, promoting a multidisciplinary approach to working with children and families integrating health, education and care. The introduction of multidisciplinary in-service degrees in Early Childhood Studies increased professional development opportunities for childcare staff. The introduction of professional status awards such as Senior Practitioner Status, Early Years Professional Status and Higher Level Teaching Assistant (HLTA) further developed vocational knowledge and skills of the early years workforce.

Foundation degrees introduced in 2000, bridged the gap between vocational and academic qualifications, a higher education award integrating work-based learning with academic rigour (QAA, 2002), safeguarding both the rigour and relevance of initial training for teachers and affording improved opportunities of in-service training for childcare workers. There had been a lack of professional development opportunities and career structures for nursery nurses (Hutchinson, 1992). The inclusion of more support staff within the school workforce in recent years highlighted the training and development needs for support staff such as teaching assistants (Simkins et al., 2009). The recommendations in the Rumbold Report (DES, 1990) drove the development of a plethora of undergraduate and FDs in Early Childhood Studies and Early Years, providing continuing professional development (CPD) opportunities for the early years workforce.

Foundation degrees contributed to the first sector-recognized professional award. The Sure Start recognized Early Years Sector-Endorsed Foundation Degree (EYSEFD) (DfES, 2001) for practitioners working with babies and young children under the age of 8 years, with a minimum of two years' vocational experience, provided opportunity for professional learning for many practitioners, especially women. Nursery nurses, teaching assistants and play workers had access to a long-awaited professional development opportunity. This higher education programme, supported by government funding, demonstrated an overdue financial investment in the early years workforce. For the first time, the predominantly female workforce had the opportunity to access higher academic study with financial support (Lumsden, 2008).

On completion of the EYSEFD, by demonstrating core and route specific outcomes, graduates were awarded the professional status of Senior Practitioner (SPS), a new level of professional practice to help raise standards and recognize experienced practitioners (DES, 2002). However, the Senior Practitioner role and responsibilities were not clearly defined (O'Keefe and Tait, 2004). The role had potential to influence practice, but was never developed. The EYSEFD now has a revised curriculum including the Common Core of Skills and Knowledge, skills and knowledge that everyone who works with children and young people is expected to have (CWDC, 2010a). The award of Senior Practitioner Status (SPS) is not given on completion of this EYSEFD; the role is generally not used or recognized, being replaced by the Early Years Professional Status (EYPS) award and the more defined role of the Early Years Professional (EYP) as a graduate professional leader of practice (Lloyd and Hallet, 2010).

The HLTA is a professional award for Teaching assistants (TAs) working in schools. On successful demonstration of standards, the award is given to TAs now able to work at a higher level with additional responsibilities, supporting the work of teachers in planning and preparation by undertaking whole class activities. The role developed from the reforming of the school workforce (DfES, 2003) to raise standards and address teachers' workloads. Through the SPS, EYPS and HLTA awards, the knowledge and skills of support staff have been raised and these professional awards have contributed to the further development of a graduate-led workforce, which is considered next.

Developing a graduate-led workforce

The EPPE Project (Sylva et al., 2010) identified a connection between the qualifications of staff in pre-school settings and outcomes for children, particularly at National Curriculum, Key Stage 1. In settings that were graduate-led by teachers, the quality of provision was higher and there were better outcomes for children. The Children's Workforce Strategy (DfES, 2005) sets out a vision of childcare services becoming among the best in the world with a better qualified workforce and more workers trained to a professional level, including all those leading full daycare provision, and where the professional level is defined as graduate level (DCSF, 2007). Schools in the maintained sector are already led by graduate-qualified teachers. Developing graduate professional leaders in the PVI sector, in children's centres and daycare provision provides parity across the maintained and non-maintained (PVI) sectors.

Reflective practice in which participants are asked to be self-reflective, and to reflect upon their professional practice with children and families, is included in professional awards, that is, the National Professional Qualification for Integrated Centre Leadership (NPQICL) for those leading integrated children's centres and the EYPS for leaders of practice in settings. Findings from the national research study about graduate leadership training (EYPS) showed that graduate-level professional development is improving setting provision and has a significant impact on a practitioner's ability to effect change (Hadfield and Waller,

2011). Government strategy supports the development of an integrated and graduate-led children's workforce through graduate-level professional leadership to help give every child the chance to thrive in their earliest years (Teather, 2011).

Developing an integrated workforce

An education is the most effective route for young children out of poverty and disaffection (Knowles, 2009), Government policies aim to close gaps in educational achievement, raise attainment and aspirations, and ensure standards of educational excellence for all. The EPPE Project found children had higher-quality care and learning experiences in pre-school settings where children are part of joined-up thinking, multidisciplinary integrated practice (Sylva et al., 2010). Recent government reviews of provision (Allen, 2011; Field 2010) identified the importance of early intervention for young children's learning and development, particularly for vulnerable and disadvantaged children, in securing better educational outcomes and life chances for children. The Tickell Review of the EYFS curriculum highlighted the importance of health and well-being for children's learning, introducing the concept of healthy learning for children's learning and development (Tickell, 2011). The Munro Review of Child Protection (Munro, 2010) brings together the interface of education, health and social services for safeguarding children. Practitioners with reflective abilities are central to implementing government policy into practice (Paige-Smith and Craft, 2011), being able to reflect upon existing provision, and modify and develop provision and practice within an emerging landscape of policy.

Traditionally, professionals in the health, education and social services have worked separately within disparate services. The delivery of more integrated services, developing 'a team around a child' to meet individual children's needs, requires new ways of working, a significant culture change for staff used to working within narrower professional or service boundaries (Siraj-Blatchford et al., 2007). There has been a broadening of job roles through the development of a range of services in establishing integrated practice, as the following job titles show:

- Children's Centre Manager
- Behaviour Education Support Team Leader
- Learning Mentor
- Family Support Worker
- Lead Professional.

The diverse roles in integrated practice enable the development of a multi-agency team around a child, meeting their individual needs. The following case study demonstrates multi-professionals working together.

 Case study: *A multi-agency team meeting*

A multi-agency team working in one of four locality areas within a large town meets for a staff meeting. The team of a probation officer, an educational psychologist, a learning mentor, a social worker, a mental health worker and a safeguarding officer are located within one building. At their weekly meeting each practitioner reports their case load. Together they discuss any emerging issues pertinent to their case load of children and families or to the local area which they serve. Their weekly meeting is a time when they can work together, pass on information, and ask for information and advice. The team working together in one building means that, through personal contact and professional understanding, relationships are established, benefiting effective communication which is central for the operation of the team and building an inter-professional service around the children and families they work with.

The case study highlighting integrated practice helps to ensure children and their families benefit from the complementary skills of a wide range of professionals working together. Multidisciplinary teams can provide well-focused access to more specialized support (DfES, 2004) and access to early intervention programmes. A joined-up service with integrated thinking involves effective two-way communication through partnership working, and trust and respect for each professional's specialism. The case study forms a basis for you to reflect upon your own integrated practice.

 Questions for reflection: *Multi-agency working*

Reflect upon an aspect of integrated practice provided for a child within your provision.

- Consider any benefits for the child and their family.
- Consider any disadvantages for the child and their family.
- What was your role in working with multi-professionals, the child and their family?

The importance of partnership working in integrated practice is now discussed.

Working in partnership

In developing a fair and just society, support and early intervention to help the most vulnerable children forms a central strand of early years policy (Teather, 2011). The Allen (2011) and Field Reports (2010) recommend intervening early for children's life chances and educational outcomes, particularly for disadvantaged children. The implementation of early intervention programmes requires practitioners to work in partnership with parents, professionals and agencies in an integrated way. The Tickell Review of the EYFS (2011) considered how children with specific needs can be supported as early as possible, highlighting the requirement for a close working relationship between practitioners in health, early years and education alongside parents and carers for early intervention strategies to be effective (Tickell, 2011).

Parents are recognized as children's first and enduring educators, regarded as key partners in supporting children's learning and development (DfES, 2008). The EYFS curriculum recognizes parents and families are central to a child's well-being; practitioners should develop this relationship by sharing information and offering support for extending learning in the home (DfES, 2008). The key person has an important role in developing this relationship, working closely with parents, as a point of contact with an individual child's parents and carers (Elfer et al., 2012). This role highlights the changing nature of practitioners' developing role and responsibilities, which are very different from the lower-skilled role of a nursery nurse 'washing the paint points'. The key-person role requires effective communication skills, observation and assessment, record-keeping and report writing (Elfer et al., 2012).

For practitioners, working with parents and other professionals within integrated practice requires an understanding of the term 'partnership'. What does it mean to work in partnership, as an equal partner? An effective partnership is based upon equality in working together; neither partner has more power in the partnership than the other. The quality of the relationship formed is central to partnership working and takes time to nurture and establish through respect and trust, so partners can ask for and share information (Draper and Duffy, 2010). This free flow of information-sharing helps a child or children, which is generally the purpose of establishing the partnership with parents, professionals or agencies. Figure 1.1 illustrates the key components discussed in a 'partnership sandwich' of practitioners working with parents and professionals effectively through trusting and nurturing relationships of respect and equity.

There is an opportunity for you to reflect upon your partnership working using the 'partnership sandwich' framework for your reflection.

Parents and Professionals
Asking
Relationships
Trust
Nurturing
Equality
Respect
Sharing
Helping
Information
Partnership

Figure 1.1   A Partnership Sandwich: practitioners working in partnership

ᔛ Questions for reflection: *A partnership sandwich*

If you are *a practitioner*, reflect upon your partnership working, either with parents, professionals or agencies.

- Give an example of partnership working from your practice.
- Reflect upon how effective the partnership is for:

  - the child or children
  - parents/carers
  - the setting
  - other professionals.

- Are there any recommendations you could make to improve future partnership working?

If you are *a student* in work placement, reflect upon your observations of partnership working; choose an example with parents, professionals or agencies.

- From observed practice reflect upon:

  - The relationship between the partners, how has this been nurtured?
  - How equal do you consider the relationship?

- Reflect upon how effective the partnership is for:

  - the child or children
  - parents/carers
  - the setting
  - other professionals.

- Are there any recommendations to improve future partnership working?

The chapter now considers the contribution of continuing professional learning for practitioners' personal and professional development and early years provision.

The contribution of professional learning

Access to higher education awards, foundation, undergraduate, postgraduate degree programmes and sector-endorsed professional awards, has enabled practitioners to engage in reflective professional learning. National findings of the EYSEFD found students who were practitioners had high levels of personal and professional confidence as they progressed through their studies (Lumsden, 2008). Similarly, students'experiences of an Early Childhood Studies undergraduate degree demonstrated a specialized knowledge and confidence within the subject (O'Keefe and Tait, 2004). The national research of graduate-level professional development (EYPS) is having a positive impact upon experienced staff and particularly early career professionals (Hadfield and Waller, 2011). These higher education professional development opportunities viewed within the context of widening participation and lifelong learning, have provided educational opportunities for those who did not pursue higher education when leaving school (Lumsden, 2008), facilitating enhanced specialized knowledge and professional confidence.

A growing self-esteem and confidence are important attributes for early childhood leaders (Rodd, 2006). The developing diversity of practitioner roles within the early years sector highlights the importance of practitioners being reflective to implement government policy into provision and practice (Paige-Smith and Craft, 2011). Research shows that professional learning has a measurable effect on the quality of children's experiences. Practitioners are able to refine their professional knowledge and skills, to enable them to respond to the increasingly complex task of providing high-quality early childhood education (Menmuir and Hughes, 1998). The research study of graduate leaders' training (EYPS) demonstrates the development of EYP leaders' growing professional confidence (Hadfield and Waller, 2011).

Through professional learning an articulate, confident workforce is leading children's services, integrated practice, setting provision and practice. The quiet 'invisible' early years workforce of nursery nurses and classroom assistants has emerged from behind the paint pots to a 'visible' workforce of leaders and managers. Practitioners who are knowledgeably confident, articulate and reflective, are leading policy, practice and change, as this graduate in the FD case study reflects at the end of her higher education studies.

Reflective practitioner's voice

I seem to walk taller; I know what I am doing and am not afraid to say so.

 ## Summary

This chapter has storied the development of roles and responsibilities of early years practitioners through the landscape of policy, practice, research and workforce reform. Working in partnership with parents and professionals in integrated practice has been considered as an emerging aspect of the developing role of the early years practitioner. Consideration of gender within the workforce has highlighted the active agency of the predominantly female early years workforce. The contribution of graduate-level professional learning upon practitioners' professional knowledge and confidence has been explored. There has been opportunity to reflect upon relevant issues and work practices through reflective questions.

The importance of reflection in continuing professional learning for early years practitioners is discussed in the following chapter.

Further reading

This report provides an analysis of issues within the early years workforce:
Cooke, G. and Lawton, K. (2008) *For Love or Money: Pay, Progression and Professionalism in the Early Years Workforce*. London: Institute for Public Policy Research.

This is an informative book about multi-agency working in the early years:
Siraj-Blatchford, I., Clarke, K. and Needham, M. (eds) (2007) *The Team Around the Child: Multi-agency Working in the Early Years*. Stoke-on-Trent: Trentham Books.

2

Being a Reflective Early Years Practitioner

Chapter overview

Early years practitioners engaging in reflective learning within their work context has enabled them to become reflective practitioners working professionally with young children, families and other professionals. There is opportunity to reflect upon your work-based reflective learning throughout the chapter.

This chapter will:
- Explore the concepts of reflective learning and practice.
- Discuss theories of reflection.
- Examine qualities and attributes of being a reflective practitioner.
- Provide ways for practitioners to reflect upon their professional practice.

Reflective learning

The early years landscape is evolving and changing due to change in government-led policy and reform and international influences upon pedagogy and practice. These influences introduce new ideas, providing opportunities for reflection to inform professional practice. As practitioners work, they see new landscapes opening up ahead, while the landscapes of policy and professional practice they have just passed through appear different as they look back. Looking back through a reflective lens informs new ways of thinking of and developing professional practice to put policy into practice (Dahlberg et al., 2007).

There is an emerging importance for early years practitioners to be reflective in the continuously changing environment within the early years sector, particularly in regard to integrated working, which requires a reflective and sensitive approach to developing new ways for multi-professional working (Paige-Smith and Craft, 2011). Early years practitioners are particularly affected in developing their practice by shifts in policy. Practitioners use practical professional knowledge to interpret and respond to changes in policy and practice (Edwards, 2000). The purpose of reflective practice is to provide better quality experiences for children and their families. When practitioners engage in reflection, they can improve provision and practice by making informed decisions about whether their work with children is effective or not (Brookfield, 1995). The quality of children's lives does not depend upon government policy, but rather on the way in which practitioners interpret the policy (Foley and Rixson, 2008) using their professional knowledge and experience to reflectively learn from, subsequently modify and improve provision for children and families, as well as developing their own professional practice as early years practitioners.

The Every Child Matters policy (DfES, 2004) introduced a significant change in approach for practitioners from working in an educational service to working with health and social care agencies in a multi-professional way for the well-being of children, developing an integrated approach to service delivery for children and young people from birth to 19 years of age. The recommendations in the Allen Review (Allen, 2011) for intervening early with support for children's learning and development rather than later, build upon the integrated practice within the Every Child Matters approach to service delivery. The following case study describes how the Deputy Manager of a Children's Centre learnt about the recommendations for early intervention strategies in the Allen Review, enabling her to reflect upon her role as Deputy Manager in implementing the recommendations within her Children's Centre. It was the start of her reflective learning for implementing Government policy into practice.

 Case study: *Early intervention strategies*

Evie noticed 'The Allen Review: recommendations for early intervention' on the agenda of her local Children's Centre Network meeting. Before going she thought, what is this 'Allen Review' and the recommendations for early intervention? Is it something else we have to do? With these thoughts rumbling in her mind, she went to the local network meeting, hoping for some clarity.

(Continued)

(Continued)

The Head of the Local Authority's Children's Services was the speaker at the meeting; she gave some background information about the Allen Review, highlighting the importance of intervening early with support services for children rather than in children's later years, as the impact for children's educational outcomes and life chances was greater. She explained the underpinning philosophy of early intervention strategies, an integrated approach to working with children and families, recognizing the individual well-being needs of every child early and building a team of professionals around the child to meet his or her education, health and social needs.

On leaving the meeting, Evie thought, this makes it clearer. I now understand what the Allen Review is about and the importance of early intervention. We already have child-centred multi-agency review meetings, run parenting classes and have outreach family support provision in our children's centre. I'll talk with Deanne the Centre Manager and discuss how we can reflect upon what we already do and build upon it to further develop early intervention strategies and integrated practice within our provision.

The case study demonstrates how reflection can inform and develop practice. Reflection provides a process for practitioners to change the landscape in which they work, with the ability to reflect and challenge existing ways of working (Reed, 2008) through reading, discussing with others, thinking about theory, research and how these relate to, and inform, practice. Reflection concerns the further reprocessing and understanding of knowledge, part of meaningful learning where the practitioner seeks to make sense of new material, linking it to what she knows already, modifying existing knowledge and meaning to develop and accommodate new ideas (Moon, 1999). This is a reorganization of knowledge and meaning into new categories of knowledge and understanding for professional practice. The process is a bit like reorganizing a filing cabinet, adding file dividers for new knowledge, as learning about topics within the Early Childhood file grows. Evie, in the case study, has added a new file divider labelled 'Early Intervention' to her filing cabinet. Practitioners' engagement in knowledge informs reflective practice. Reflective practice within the framework of work-based reflective learning is now discussed.

Work-based reflective practice

Reflective learning and work-based learning are interrelated, both potentially powerful pedagogy for transformational change in practice

(Foundation Degree Forward, 2005), transforming learning at and from work, *through* the development of reflective learning abilities (Moon, 2006). Reflective practice, or practice that has been considered, has been likened to looking *in* a mirror and looking *through* a window (Jones and Pound, 2008). When looking in a mirror at practice, it is like looking at yourself in a mirror – the reflection is one way and only one image is seen. Considering practice, the reflection about practice is introspective and inward looking. When looking through a window upon practice, reflection has a wider view, with many different perspectives and ways of seeing provision and practice, providing more opportunities to reflect, review, modify, extend and develop professional practice. Biggs (1999: 6) further explains reflection using the mirror metaphor: 'reflection in professional practice, however, gives back not what it is, but what might be, an improvement on the original'. Practical experience is essential for developing expertise, but is not in itself sufficient (Maynard and Thomas, 2009); it is only when practitioners assimilate different ways of thinking and working that they can gain more progression in their own views and ways of working. It is through engaging in reading, research, professional development activity and reflective dialogue with colleagues and other professionals that practitioners acquire the characteristics of the 'reflective practitioner' (Schon, 2007).

Reflective practice should encourage practitioners to 'feel' their work, an approach that goes beyond observation but challenges knowledge and practice, moving to a place of understanding (Leeson, 2010: 181). Personal and professional self-knowledge gained through reflection can be unnerving, not everyone is prepared to take the risk and critically unpick their professional practice and their work as a practitioner. After reflection, modifying professional practice can be just as challenging and the process of reflective learning within reflective practice can be emotionally demanding. It is important to strike a balance between being reflective and professionally self-critical without being overly negative, which can be professionally destructive.

The reflective practitioner

The early years workforce is in a process of continuous change, as discussed in Chapter 1. What kind of workforce is required to work within the landscape of emerging policy and practice? What qualities and attributes should practitioners have to work effectively with young children, parents and other professionals?

How does reflection contribute to the development of an effective workforce?

Moss (2011) envisages a workforce with professional qualities of ethical and value-based reflective practice. Being reflective and being a reflective practitioner concern qualities and attributes in a person's behaviour, rather than a cognitive activity, a process of seeing and being that is part of the professional way an early years practitioner works, thinks and behaves (Paige-Smith and Craft, 2011). Moss (2008b: 125) further defines such a practitioner as 'a democratic reflective professional', an early childhood worker who is a critical thinker and researcher, a co-constructor of meaning, with identity and values, who values participation, diversity and dialogue. A practitioner with a self-reflecting pedagogy, able to engage in democratic discourse with others, through reflection develops a sense of self (Dalhberg et al., 2007). The emerging 'sense of self' as an early years professional workforce is discussed later in Chapter 7.

Reflective behaviour concerns attributes and qualities demonstrated in practitioners' interactions with children, parents and colleagues. These include the ability to reason, problem solve and find solutions; evaluate and discuss issues; give constructive feedback and be able to receive feedback from others; learn from others; explain values and pedagogical beliefs; consider others' views, theories, pedagogy and research and to think in a reflective way to improve provision and practice. The REFLECT (Reason, Evaluate, Feedback, Learn, Explain, Consider, Think) Framework in Figure 2.1 illustrates some of these reflective attributes and qualities.

- **Reason**

- **Evaluate**

- **Feedback**

- **Learn**

- **Explain**

- **Consider**

- **Think**

Figure 2.1   The REFLECT Framework

〰️ **Questions for reflection:** *The REFLECT Framework*

There is opportunity for you to consider your own reflective behaviour using the REFLECT Framework.

Consider your work over the last week and the reflective behaviour you used in your interactions with children, parents and professionals. How have you:

- Reasoned or solved a problem?
- Evaluated your work?
- Given feedback to a colleague or received feedback from a colleague?
- Learnt something new?
- Explained to a child, parent or colleague?
- Considered – a new idea? A colleague's point of view?
- Thought – made time and space to think reflectively?

Theories of reflective practice

The concept of reflective practice and being a 'reflective practitioner' concerns how professionals think in their practice (Schon, 2007) through defining two processes of reflection:

- reflection *in* practice
- reflection *on* practice.

These terms highlight two levels of reflective practice. An early years practitioner may reflect *in* their practice by thinking about the activities they undertake with children as they carry them out. An early years practitioner who reflects *on* their practice, away from the physical activity of doing it, takes the reflective process to a higher level, by linking practice to theories, developing 'theories in use' and new ways of working (Schon, 2007). This reflective process and behaviour develops and expands professional knowledge and practice. Being a reflective practitioner is a characteristic of a person's behaviour rather than an intellectual activity (Moon, 2006).

Early years practitioners undertake routine tasks daily, without really thinking about why or how they are carried out. Reflective practice is a change agent for practitioners to modify, develop, improve or change provision for children. The following case study illustrates Schon's theory of reflective practice within an early years context; a Foundation Stage teacher in a primary school reflects upon the daily routine of children lining up.

📁 **Case study: *Children lining up***

Asking children to 'line up' is a frequent request made by teachers and practitioners, sometimes several times a day.

Reflecting in practice

Amera is a newly qualified Foundation Stage teacher; she 'herded' her class of 30 children several times during the day by asking them to 'line up'. The children lined up to go out to play, to go into assembly, to wash their hands before dinner, to go into the book corner for story time and to go home. Amera observed at these times, the children were herded like animals into small spaces. As a result, the children behaved in aggressive ways, pushing, pulling and poking each other. She ended up raising her voice above the children's noise, to manage the crowd of children and to keep them safe. This was a stressful time for the children and herself each day. What could she do to improve the situation, so it was calmer and more enjoyable for all?

Reflecting on practice

Amera remembered a comment made by a special needs adviser who attended her school. Teachers and practitioners tend to see a child's inappropriate behaviour and reprimand them for this, but it is not always the child's fault. We should look at the environment we create for children and consider the activity we ask them to do.

At break time as Amera drank her cup of coffee in the staffroom, she looked up at the shelf of books and she noticed a book about managing young children's behaviour. In reading this, Amera realized the importance of creating an environment in which successful behaviour can take place. A key strategy in behaviour management is to develop preventative approaches. Amera reflected that the daily routine of children lining up was developing into a behaviour management issue. She reflected upon her reading, what is my preventative strategy? She realized she did not have one, so devised a different approach to the routine of children lining up.

She decided to ask the children to line up in small groups, selecting the groups of four children in different ways. For example, she would invite: anyone who is wearing yellow, can line up; anyone whose name begins with an 's', can line up; anyone who is wearing stripes, can line up. Lining up in small groups would prevent the mass herding of children, and the inappropriate behaviours she had experienced, allowing the space in front of the door to slowly fill with children, rather than be filled all at once.

The next day Amera tried this approach out. The children listened expectantly to hear what she called out, would it belong to them? When it did, they jumped up and ran to the door to line up, standing quietly to see who would join them. On her way home Amera reflected upon her day . . . lining up in smaller groups had benefited children's behaviour, the children were calmer and she felt calmer too.

In the case study, Amera identified an aspect of her practice to review and modify by reflecting upon her practice, and then she modified a daily routine.

 Questions for reflection: *Reviewing your practice*

Consider an aspect of your practice that you have reviewed and modified.

- How has reflection enabled you to modify, change or improve practice?
- How have children, parents, staff benefited?
- How have you as a practitioner benefited?

Theories of reflection

In the process of reflection, it is important to start from where the child is (Samuelson and Carlsson, 2008), to see the world through young children's eyes, the starting point for reflection. For reflection to be meaningful, it is important to identify the specific aspect of practice, which may be identifying a problem, to reflect upon and learn about it, with the aim of changing and improving provision and practice for the better. Schon (2007) and Dewey (1933) view reflection as a process of problem solving, the reflection begins when practitioners identify issues as problems within their provision and practice. An issue of practice may be seen as a problem by one practitioner and not by another, however an unidentified problem cannot be acted upon (Loughran, 2002).

Dewey (1933) identifies three attitudes as important for fostering reflective thinking: open-mindedness, responsibility and wholeheartedness. Practitioners who are 'open-minded' are willing to accept other perspectives, able to accept the possibility that their views and practices can be developed in light of other viewpoints. Other perspectives are gained through reading academic literature, journal articles about research, conversations with other professionals, visiting other settings, and attending network meetings and short and long courses.

Responsibility is part of reflective thinking. Practitioners with a responsible attitude are actively engaged in thinking about children in the broadest sense, not only thinking about what they are doing in their practice, but also considering factors beyond; for example, how will any change in practice resulting from their reflective thinking impact upon children's learning outcomes, or service delivery? The third of Dewey's attitudes, 'wholeheartedness' enables practitioners to be genuinely reflective, to have reflective agency for change, not only for the children and families they work with, but within the wider landscape of national, local and regional early years contexts for policy, provision and practice.

Hatton and Smith (1995) regard reflection as deliberate thinking about action with the view to improvement. Critical reflection is the ability to understand the wider social and political functions of experience and meaning-making and apply this understanding in wider social contexts (Fook, 2010). Dewey (1933) regards a reflective practitioner as a reflectively persistent one, engaging in continuous consideration of their underlying beliefs and knowledge, considering other beliefs and knowledge to illuminate their own values, beliefs and working practices. Dewey's notion of continuous reflection has relevance for the changing world of early years and childcare (Miller et al., 2005).

Pollard et al. (2002) describe aspects of the process of reflection within the framework of reflective practice. Reflection should include: a focus on goals, with consideration of how they are addressed and achieved; searching for evidence from practice as the main source of information for reflection; being open-minded with an inclusive attitude; modifying existing practice from insights from reading, research and prior reflections; having regular dialogue with colleagues; reflecting according to the situation; and realizing when to change practice or to keep existing practice. For reflection to be meaningful, it is important to consider what aspect of provision and practice to reflect upon and the level of reflection to engage in.

Van Manen (1977) broadens the meaning of reflection for practitioners, enabling them to reflect beyond their own professional practice. He suggests reflection has three levels: technical rationality, practical action of reflection and critical reflection. At the first level, reflection concerns techniques as a means to an end, to produce efficiency and effectiveness. Practitioners are mainly concerned with immediate effectiveness without considering how the goal or target was achieved. At the second level, 'practical reflection', practitioners think about the quality of the educational process. Practitioners using the third level of 'critical reflection' begin to think about wider social or educational implications beyond their own practice.

These theories of reflective practice are represented in a model of reflective learning in Figure 2.2. The model illustrates the essence of

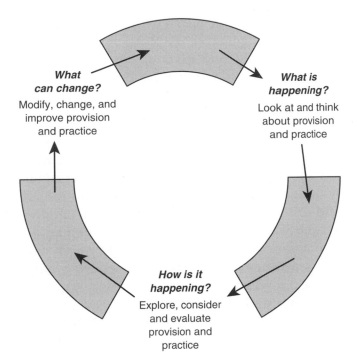

What can change?
Modify, change, and improve provision and practice

What is happening?
Look at and think about provision and practice

How is it happening?
Explore, consider and evaluate provision and practice

Figure 2.2 Reflective Learning: a reflective cycle for improvement and change

the theories of reflection within a reflective cycle for improvement and change, highlighting the role of the practitioner in reflectively evaluating provision and practice.

The three questions in the model provide layers of reflection.

- *What is happening?* A descriptive overview of provision and practice.
- *How is it happening?* A more in-depth analysis of provision and practice.
- *What can change?* Information from the two questions above informs the practitioner about what aspect of provision and practice they can modify, change or improve for better health, social and educational outcomes for children and families.

Reflective learning to improve provision and practice

Figure 2.2 provides a framework for reflective improvement and change. Practical ways of reflective learning used in early years contexts are now considered.

Reflective documentation, dialogue, questions and writing are ways for practitioners to individually and collectively engage in reflection, to learn about the children they work with, the provision and practice they provide, or about themselves as early years practitioners. Reflective learning provides a catalyst for personal and professional enhancement, and improvement in provision and practice.

Reflective documentation and dialogue

Documentation as pedagogy for reflective dialogue is used in pre-schools in the Reggio Emilia region in northern Italy. Pedagogues allocate time and space to meet together to reflect upon children's learning. By using a broad range of documentation such as video, tape recording and written notes, they discuss how their children are learning. Their reflective discussion around the documentation makes visible the learning processes and strategies used by each child (Rinaldi, 2005). There is a different emphasis in assessing young children's learning in these pre-schools than in some nursery schools in England. The Early Years Foundation Stage curriculum used in England is concerned with what children learn, recording children's learning as outcomes, rather than documenting the process of children's learning and using the documentation for discussion to understand how individual children learn, as in the pre-schools in Reggio Emilia.

Some pre-school settings in England have been influenced by reflective pedagogy and practices used in Reggio Emilia pre-schools. The introduction of accessible digital technology has enabled practitioners to use photographs for children to recall and reflect upon their learning, and for practitioners to have reflective conversations with the children and their parents, as the case study shows.

 Case study: *Reflective documentation*

Hannah is a Lead Practitioner working in a small nursery school attached to a primary school in a rural location. She explains how observation and photographs are used within her nursery to inform planning for children's learning.

> We always say observation and reflection are part of our central strategy of how we teach and help children learn here. We observe the children through photographs, observing, writing things down and just generally being with them. At the end of the session, we always show the photos to the children in a slide show, displayed on the nursery wall. We have the photos printed off and stuck into their own diaries which they take home with them every day, so the parents can see them. The parents do the same, they put things in the diaries for us as well, so that forms a central hub of what we see.

> Then as practitioners with the children we reflect on what the children have done. Quite often the children will say we did that today, we'd like to do that tomorrow, extending it in their own way. As practitioners, we also say, they were fantastic at that, for example like George who made his cake today, how can we extend this for him? Can we include some more children or where can it go next? The observation really feeds the reflection and the reflection feeds into our planning. It's a cycle, all the time encompassing everything we do.

The case study highlights the importance of professional conversations and reflective writing as key elements in reflective learning and practice and, importantly, the creation of time and space for reflective thinking and dialogue to take place. This has been created in the daily meetings for the nursery team to meet to reflect upon the learning that has taken place during the day.

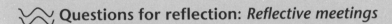

Questions for reflection: *Reflective meetings*

Consider your own work setting or work placement.

- When do you have time to meet together?
- What is the agenda for the meetings?
- Do you have time to reflect upon children's progress in the meetings?
- Do you have time to meet with children to share and reflect upon their learning?
- Do you have time when you can meet with parents to share and reflect upon their child's progress?
- How effective are the meetings?
- Are there any recommendations for improvement?

Nursery teams working together are reflective professional practitioners (Moss, 2008b) engaging in dialogue with others from a knowledgeable value base of early years principles and practice. Reflective practitioners have agency to change and improve provision and practice (Osgood, 2006). By personal and professional responsibility for the outcomes of children, practitioners use their personal and professional attributes and qualities to be part of a 'community of practice' (Wenger, 1998: 10) to make meaning, construct theories and testing them through listening and dialogue with others, then reconstructing those theories (Moss, 2008b). This process of reflective practice has similarities to Reggio Emilia's pedagogy of listening (Rinaldi, 2005)

within a reflective culture of a learning community where pedagogues actively listen, engage in dialogue and make meaning with
others about children's learning (Reed and Canning, 2010).

Reflective questions

The use of questioning in professional dialogue is central for reflective
learning to take place. It is important for early years practitioners to
work in a questioning culture in which provision and practice can be
examined through a critical learning dialogue (Hallet, 2008b). The use
of questioning guides reflection, further learning and finds solutions.
The five words listed below, used as a Questions Guide, support and
enable practitioners' reflection:

What?
 • Is the focus for reflection?
How?
 • Will the reflection be used?
Who?
 • Will take part in the reflection?
 • Will benefit from the reflection?
When?
 • Time – when will reflection take place?
Where?
 • Space – where is the best venue for reflection?

   The use of questioning to solve emerging issues and problems, and
within a cycle of review, evaluation and planning, provides a framework for reflective review and evaluation of provision and practice.
The Review, Evaluate and Plan (REP) framework uses these five questions for reflection:

Review
 • Ask the 'What' question – to identify the emerging issue or
   problem.
Evaluate
 • Ask the 'How' question – to solve the emerging issue or problem,
   who or what resources could help me solve the problem?
Plan
 • Ask the 'When' question – to provide a timescale to solve the
   emerging issue or problem.

〰️ **Questions for reflection:** *The REP framework*

You are asked to identify an aspect of your practice that you are concerned about in your work as a practitioner, or that you have seen as a student in your work placement. Using the REP framework, reflect upon your practice and the process of reflective learning.

Review

- What aspect of practice are you considering?
- What emerging issue or problem do you wish to reflect upon?

Evaluate

- How can I find a solution?
- What knowledge or skills do I require?
- Who could help me?
- What resources could help me?

Plan

- What is the time scale for improving the issue or solving the problem?
- What is the time line?
- What are the short-term actions required?
- What are the long-term goals required?

Now consider the process of reflective learning. What have you learnt about:

- Addressing emerging issues and solving problems in provision and practice?
- Engaging in reflection?
- Planning for improving provision and practice?
- Yourself as a reflective learner?

Reflective writing

Throughout their work, early years practitioners write in different formats, such as school or setting evaluation reports, development and improvement plans, staff appraisal notes and children's records. All these have a specific genre of writing and are for a particular audience, an Office for Standards in Education (Ofsted) inspector, school governors, colleagues, parents and other agencies. The activity of writing provides a vehicle and space for reflective thinking, learning and practice.

Narrative writing in journals and diaries provides opportunity for personal and professional reflection. The use of narrative writing and storying is a powerful way for practitioners to make sense of their experiences (Bolton, 2010) in a reflective way. Reflective dialogue, documentation and writing are ways to enable practitioners to engage in reflective practice as reflective practitioners. The following case study demonstrates this.

 Case study: *Being a reflective practitioner*

Claire is a nursery teacher working in a primary school. She considers herself as a reflective practitioner and encourages reflective dialogue within her nursery team. She writes about this in an essay as part of her postgraduate study:

> Children need more than our enthusiasm. They need us as practitioners to think about what we are doing and why. Reflective practice has a deeply positive impact on setting provision. It ensures continuing professional development, deepens understanding of learning, supports planning, improves further pedagogical work and blurs the boundaries between research, theory and practice. A reflective practitioner is able to accept their subjectivity as strength and to embrace uncertainty as an opportunity to research and create new understandings and meaning through dialogue with others. In a landscape of shifting social and political contexts, reflective practice enables practitioners to maintain the continuous cycle of interpretation and response that is necessary when faced with complex and unique situations; this will ensure effective change and development in setting provision.
>
> There are numerous challenges to the nurturing of reflective practice; making time and space to reflect on our practice is of concern; how to document and share information about children's learning and our own reflections in and on practice. Perhaps the most significant of these challenges is to remain open. By remaining open to new perspectives, approaches and insights from others we enable a dialogue and facilitate the forging of new perspectives and understandings through collaborative meaning-making.

The case study shows how higher education studies have influenced Claire in being a reflective practitioner and leading reflective pedagogy within her nursery. Similarly this FD graduate from the case study considers her development as a reflective early years practitioner through her work-based studies.

Reflective practitioner's voice

It's made me think about things more. I now unpick what I do with children to understand more.

Summary

The chapter has explored the notion of reflection in its broadest sense, by examining theories of reflection, reflective learning and practice. These have been considered within frameworks for improvement and change. The concept of reflective practitioners behaving in a reflective way has been examined within the context of the early years. Through case studies and suggestions of how practitioners can be reflective within the work setting, reflective learning, abilities and behaviours within professional practice have been considered.

Further reading

This is comprehensive book about reflective practice:
Paige-Smith, A. and Craft, A. (2011) *Developing Reflective Practice in the Early Years.* 2nd edn. Maidenhead: Open University Press.

This is seminal book about the concept of a reflective practitioner:
Schon, D.A. (1983) *The Reflective Practitioner: How Professionals Think in Action.* New York: Basic Books.

3

Work-based Reflective Learning

Chapter overview

Work-based reflective learning as a process for reflective change in provision and practice is discussed within this chapter. The relationship with work-based learning and reflection is illustrated in a model of 'work-based reflective learning', demonstrating the process of reflective learning within the work context of professional practice within the early years. There is opportunity to use the model of work-based reflective learning to reflect upon your practice.

This chapter will:
- Examine work-based learning.
- Explore the concept of work-based reflective learning through a model of reflective change.
- Consider the contribution of work-based reflective learning as a process for change in provision and practice.
- Consider the transformational contribution of work-based reflective learning for practitioners' professional learning and development.

Work-based learning

Work-based learning builds upon historical and existing delivery of vocational qualifications in further and higher education, in which work-related experience is undertaken by students through work placements, work experience or sandwich courses to learn about the world of work and employment. The understanding of 'work' can have several meanings, generally understood as the place where individuals are employed to carry out activity different to that carried out in the home. Secondary school students undertake 'work experience' to experience the daily routine of work and the skills required to engage in the world of work (Cairns and Malloch, 2011). Students studying Early Childhood courses in further and higher education attend 'work placement' in nurseries, schools and early years settings, and develop an understanding of how early years settings are organized by working alongside teachers and practitioners. They often carry out activities with children to understand how children learn and develop.

Work experience and work-based learning can be viewed as two extremes on the continuum of work-related learning as they provide different levels of learning (Moon, 2006). Work-based learning concerns any learning which derives from the experience of engaging in work, however it is the nature of the relationship between work and learning that is important. Work-based learning expands work experience for students as the work activity becomes the curriculum and potentially a powerful pedagogy that is capable of transforming learning at and from work (Foundation Degree Forward, 2005) through the development of practitioners' reflective learning abilities (Moon, 2006). Wenger (2011: 9) regards learning as an organic process belonging to 'the realm of experience and practice' as knowledge is often created in action rather than before action (Marsick and Watkins, 1999). The workplace is a valid learning place where activities and interactions between the activity of work and those who work there take place (Allix, 2011) and the work context transforms learning in a creative process (Hager, 2011).

Learning as an activity involves change and development in individuals and the organizations in which they work (Cairns and Malloch, 2011). Work-based learning is a significant and inspiring element within the whole dimension of learning. The learning context of work has pedagogical properties (Allix, 2011) for work-based learning is about relationships between the processes of working and learning, recognizing that 'learning is inherent in work and work in learning' (Jacobs and Park, 2009: 150). Work-based learning starts within the work setting and, through daily practice, work-based knowledge can be used to deepen further knowledge, understanding, and academic and vocational learning. It is important for learners to re-contextualize their knowledge, transferring it to new work and academic contexts (Evans et al., 2011) to modify and improve provision and practice.

Work-based learning in higher education

In higher education there has been a tension between vocational learning (practical and applied), and academic learning (theoretical and conceptual) and relating theory to practice. Work-based learning brings together theory and practice in a pedagogical approach to vocational learning and practice as found in foundation degrees. Foundation degrees were introduced in 2000 to create a vocational route in higher education attempting to bridge the academic and vocational divide in programme delivery, challenging the traditional academic approach to undergraduate degree provision in a ground-breaking way (Beaney, 2006).

The pedagogy of work-based learning is central to FDs, making it a unique higher education award, integrating work-based learning with academic rigour through close collaboration with employers and programme providers, to equip learners with relevant knowledge and skills for the workplace (QAA, 2004). The design of the FD integrates academic learning with work-based learning and practice through college- and university-based delivery and work-based activity and assessment. Foundation degrees are delivered in further education colleges, higher education institutions and in work locations such as schools. The knowledge gained in the classroom is only one aspect of education, as experience and practice are important elements of education (Schon, 1995). Foundation degrees integrate knowledge, experience and professional practice through reflection for reflective learning within work-based contexts.

Work-based reflective learning

Nursery nurses and teaching assistants studying FDs are developing personally and professionally through the work-based element of their undergraduate studies (Rawlings, 2008). Reflection is an integrated aspect of work-based learning, however, work-based learning is usually written about in an isolated way without referring to its reflective aspect. The concept of reflective practice in work and the professions is a strand of work-based learning (Costley, 2011). Reflection enables an individual practitioner to reflect upon their daily work and learn from it. Reflection enables organizations to change and develop through collective reflection (Boud and Solomon, 2003). For effective collaborative reflection, the school, setting or service should provide conditions to support reflective learning where group reflection can take place through dialogue providing formal and informal reflective time and spaces in a climate of openness and trust. Staff and team meetings, peer mentoring, non-contact time and a comfortable staffroom where staff can chat over a cup of coffee are examples of reflective opportunities for staff to make sense of work; by giving meaning they contribute to organizational stability and development (Costley, 2011). Reflective learning is a characteristic of reflection, reflective writing and reflective practice are processes of reorganizing knowledge for further insights to modify and develop provision and practice (Moon, 2006). Reflective learning is both an individual and a collective activity.

The term 'work-based reflective learning' conceptualizes the interaction between work-based learning and reflection. This forms the pedagogy of the FD case study, discussed later in Chapter 6, and has informed the model of Work-based Reflective Learning illustrated in Figure 3.1, discussed later in this chapter. Graduates in the FD case study understood the close interrelationship between work-based learning and reflective practice, as this insight from a graduate practitioner shows:

Reflective practitioner's voice

There is a link with reflective practice and work-based learning, not everyone reflects on their practice. They can tell you what they do but they often can't reflect on it. Reflective practice extends your practice by questioning it, the 'how' and 'why' questions and, reflecting and thinking about how to change. Work-based learning is about doing and learning. Reflective practice pulls you up another level to a different dimension. Both are on a similar theme.

This reflective practitioner highlights how reflective learning carried out in the work context provides opportunity for personal and professional change, for practitioners. The practitioner describes how reflective practice 'pulls you up to another level', highlighting the development of early years practitioners' personal and professional self-confidence through work-based reflective learning.

Reflective practice provides individual or group change, development for the self and for an early years setting, school or service (Cairns and Malloch, 2011). A work-based assignment undertaken by a practitioner in his or her FD studies can influence change in provision and practice, as the following case study shows.

 Case study: *Creative time and space*

Peter is a nursery nurse working in a nursery unit within a primary school. In studying children's creativity, he observed the provision for children's creativity in his work setting. In the Creative Area of the nursery, there were art materials for the children to use; paper, paint, pencils, crayons, felt tipped pens, scissors, collage materials, glue, junk boxes, cardboard rolls, play dough and clay. Peter realized the nursery views children's creativity as painting and drawing. This narrow perspective was also limited in time and space. In using

(Continued)

(Continued)

the Creative Area there was an emphasis for children to produce an end-product, a painting, a model to take home or for display in the nursery.

This approach encouraged children to use the Creative Area quickly for production, rather than as a space for creativity. The absence of shelving prevented children from leaving a junk or clay model to return to for considered additions or amendments. Children's clay models were crumpled and returned to the clay bucket for further use. Peter began to reflect upon the provision he observed:

- Does this provision enable children's creativity?
- Does the Creative Area echo the work space of an artist who drafts, makes, considers and modifies their work in a creativity process of reflection, consideration and making?

Through his studies, Peter became familiar with the pedagogy for children's creativity in the pre-schools in Reggio Emilia, a region in northern Italy that regards each child as a creative child, with a hundred languages to express themselves, through dance, drama, role play, sculpture, music, song, poetry and story-writing. He wanted to broaden his nursery's perspective of creativity and foster an understanding of creativity as a process for learning within the nursery provision. He discussed with the nursery teacher his understanding of children's creative learning and for the nursery to facilitate more time and space for children's creativity. The provision of shelving in the Creative Area would physically develop the space. He found the price of shelving and the nursery teacher approved the purchase of shelving fixed at heights children could reach. The children were able to put their models on the shelves and return to them the next day. They now spent longer in the Creative Area, engaged in the process of creativity in a more sustained way.

Peter's work-based reflective learning began by observing provision. Observation allows practitioners time and space for reflective looking, allowing the unfamiliar to become illuminated and a catalyst for change in practice. Peter used his newly found knowledge about creative pedagogy in Reggio Emilia provision to reflect upon his own nursery's provision and make recommendations to improve practice which he articulated to the nursery teacher. Peter's reflective learning was an integrated cycle of:

Observation – **reflection** – knowledge – **reflection** –
recommendation(s) – change

Using this integrated reflective cycle consider your own practice.

Questions for reflection: *Reflective cycle*

For practitioners:

- Consider how you use observation to reflect upon practice in your work setting.
- What change in pedagogy, provision or practice occurred?

For students:

- Consider how you use observation to reflect upon practice in your work placement.
- What change in pedagogy, provision or practice do you recommend?

Model of Work-based Reflective Learning: a reflective cycle of change

The model of Work-based Reflective Learning shown in Figure 3.1 developed from the FD case study and demonstrates the interaction of work-based learning, reflection, professional practice and theory. The following FD graduate's comment shows the interface between all these elements, furthered within the model of Work-based Reflective Learning, in a reflective cycle of change.

Reflective practitioner's voice

The foundation degree is practice based. The work-based element is important to help you reflect on what you do every day and to link theory and relate it to work-based practice. I started with my practice and then got to the theory. It's a cycle, how theory fits into practice and how to modify it. I read the theory to understand what I do. For practitioners in practice it valued what you did.

This graduate's reflection of her FD studies illuminates the importance of work-based learning in linking practice to theory within a reflective cycle for change.

The model in Figure 3.1 illustrates this process of work-based reflective learning. Through the spiral of reflection, there are three strands of contributory influences; employment experience, vocational and theoretical reflection, and reflective conversations. These

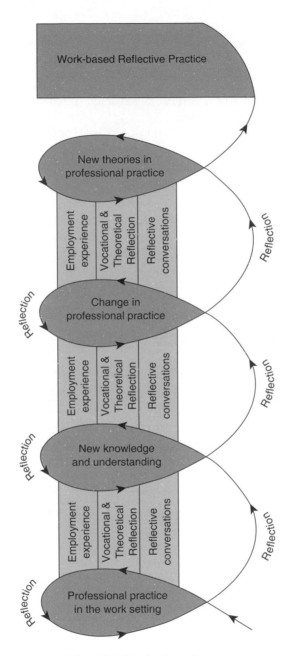

Figure 3.1   Model of Work-based Reflective Learning

are threaded through the reflective process of new learning, change in professional practice and the development of new theories in professional practice, forming work-based reflective practice.

Reflective learning begins within professional practice undertaken in the work setting. It is through reflecting upon professional practice that new knowledge and understanding are gained by vocational and theoretical reflection. For example, by reading vocationally professional magazines and journals, academic literature, research journals and reports, and engaging in reflective conversations with others, and through employment experience of working in the early years sector. The knowledge and understanding gained are reflectively fed back to inform change in professional practice. Again, this is reflected upon and generates new theories to use in practice. This reflective cycle of thinking and behaving constitutes work-based reflective learning for reflective practice.

Work-based reflective learning for practitioners

It is through the development of new theories and ways of working within professional practice that work-based reflective learning becomes a powerful vehicle for practitioners' personal and professional development, their self-confidence and self-esteem increased through newly found knowledge about practice which then informs their pedagogy and practice. Practitioners *seem to walk taller* through their higher education studies, as this FD graduate reflects.

Reflective practitioner's voice

The foundation degree is about work. It's given me confidence. I can do it. I can stand my ground. I seem to walk taller. It's a fantastic achievement. It gives you the belief 'I can do it'. It makes you feel that you are an equal to everyone in the school.

The following case study demonstrates the Model of Work-based Reflective Learning showing how work-based reflective learning influences change in pedagogy, provision and practice within an early years context, through the different elements in the model.

 Case study: *Work-based Reflective Learning: show me*

Employment experience

Hilary is a qualified teacher and the Literacy Co-ordinator in a primary school, she works in the Reception Team with another teacher and a teaching assistant in an open-plan Reception Base with 60 children.

(Continued)

(Continued)

Professional practice in the work setting

In teaching young children, Hilary is aware of the importance of children's literacy development, for a child being able to read unlocks the literate world in which they live. The approach to the teaching of reading in the school is predominantly through phonics, word recognition and a reading scheme. Phonics is taught in a systematic way, beginning with initial sounds recognition and key words, such as 'and', 'the', 'like', are taught through memory recognition. Hilary works daily with Ben who is having difficulty in recognizing the 26 initial sounds of the alphabet. She reflects . . . why was Ben having difficulty when other children were not? Was this an appropriate teaching approach for Ben?

Vocational and theoretical reflection

Hilary is studying part-time for a postgraduate diploma and learning about different approaches to the teaching of reading. Through her reading she is influenced by the work of Nigel Hall. His pedagogy of emergent literacy highlighted the importance of the environment as an enabling agency for young children's reading and writing to emerge and develop (Gillen and Hall, 2003) and for children to write in meaningful play contexts with purpose and audience. Literacy contexts such as the home corner, a café, a shop, a garage in the outside area provide playful reading and writing opportunities for young children (Brock and Ranklin, 2008). The importance of environmental print for children's early literacy learning (Hallet, 2008a) was highlighted by Hall, he included environmental print in the home corner, making a playful literate environment with resources such as calendars, recipe books, magazines, newspapers, pens and notebooks for children to engage in meaningful literacy actions.

Hilary read the work of Liz Waterland and her 'Apprenticeship Approach to Reading with Storybooks' using narrative contexts to inspire children to read and develop a positive attitude towards books and reading (Waterland, 1988). The 'Reading with Storybooks Approach' to the teaching of reading promoted a love and enjoyment of books through the context of pictures and whole stories, rather than a skill based phonics approach to reading. Hilary's professional knowledge was enhanced by attending conferences in which Hall and Waterland spoke about their pedagogies.

Her course tutor arranged for students to visit an infant school to see the use of emergent literacy pedagogy in practice. At the school, Hilary saw a rich literate environment as soon as she entered. The high visibility of books in a library in the school entrance area for parents to read with their child and to borrow, immediately signposted the importance of literacy within the school's pedagogy. This was echoed throughout the school in the range of literacy resources for children to engage with in outdoor and indoor play areas, for example, catalogues, posters, maps, writing materials, clip boards, chalks and chalking boards, plastic letters, class made photographic books. These resources were all within meaningful contexts for children to develop literacy knowledge and understanding, providing opportunities for children to read and to write.

Reflective conversations

Engaging in reflective dialogue enables practitioners to critically think through ideas and test ideas, theories and practice with others (Moss, 2008b). During the visit to the school, Hilary was able to discuss the school's pedagogy for literacy with the head teacher, teachers and with students from her class. These reflective conversations within a community of practice (Wenger, 1998) answered questions she had, furthered her understanding and developed her confidence in articulating her redefined pedagogy for children's literacy learning.

New knowledge and understanding

Hilary had gained new knowledge and understanding about young children's literacy learning through her continuing professional development course, reading about pedagogies in the teaching of literacy, attending conferences, visiting a school to observe pedagogies in practice, and by talking with others about her newly found knowledge and understanding. In reflecting about Ben and his struggle with learning initial sounds, with her new insights, she realized her school's approach to the teaching of reading was de-contextualized, rather than using a contextualized and meaningful approach to inspire children to read.

Change in professional practice

Hilary realized that through her new knowledge and understanding her pedagogy to the teaching of literacy had changed, prompting a change in her professional practice. However, she worked in a Reception Team with another teacher and a nursery nurse, sharing the teaching area, and a change in pedagogy would mean a change in teaching approach for them also. Hilary met with them, articulating her newly found pedagogy, and her teaching colleague agreed to work in the same way, supported by the nursery nurse for consistency in literacy teaching for the children in the Reception Base.

New theories in professional practice

In introducing her new pedagogy to literacy teaching, Hilary would lead by example, demonstrating the effectiveness of the approach, with the view of developing it into school policy throughout the primary school. For this she required some new resources, mainly picture and story books and other resources such as plastic letters, clipboards, chalking boards. The head teacher was the budget holder, Hilary had convinced her teaching colleague of using an emergent approach to literacy, the head teacher had a junior school background and would require more convincing. Hilary had a meeting with her, articulating her pedagogy and argument for change in policy and practice. Her head teacher listened and asked questions, being half convinced she offered a small budget for resources saying 'OK, show me … ' These words empowered Hilary, giving her permission to change pedagogy with younger children in the Reception Base.

(Continued)

(Continued)

Over the school year, the change was like a pebble in water, rippling influence through the nursery and infant departments. At the start of the next school year, there was a firm foundation of teachers and practitioners with sufficient knowledge and understanding of emergent literacy pedagogy to inform and influence teachers' pedagogy with older children in the junior department of the primary school. Over a year, through a series of staff meetings, reflective challenge and discussion took place and Hilary led the development of the school's literacy policy with staff.

Work-based reflective practice

Hilary's work-based reflective learning arose from her everyday work activity, several key events within Hilary's work context enabled her to reflect upon her practice:

- Her everyday work activity of teaching initial sounds to Reception children.
- Her continuing professional learning about the teaching of reading on her higher education course, which allowed her time and space to reflect upon provision and practice.
- Her visit to an infant school to see emergent literacy pedagogy in practice.
- Her reflective conversations with knowledgeable others.
- Her confidence and articulation of pedagogy with others, including a senior and leader budget holder.
- Her demonstration of pedagogy in professional practice.
- Her leadership of pedagogy into policy with others.

 A further case study about children's early literacy learning through play is given in Chapter 10.

Using the Model of Work-based Reflective Learning in Figure 3.1 consider your own reflective learning within your work context. The questions will help you to engage with all elements of the model in a spiral of reflective thinking and learning embedded within your daily work.

〰 Questions for reflection: *Work-based Reflective Learning*

Professional practice in the work setting

- What aspect of professional practice do you want to reflect upon?
- Why do you want to change this?

- How will the reflective change benefit the child, children, parents or staff you work with?
- How will the reflective change benefit the setting or service you work in?
- What will you learn about yourself as a practitioner through the reflective process?

New knowledge and understanding

- What new knowledge and understanding about pedagogy, provision and practice have you gained?
- How have you developed new knowledge and understanding?
- How will it inform your professional practice?

Change in professional practice

- How will you implement change in your own professional practice?
- How will you influence others?

New theories in professional practice

- What new theory/theories have you developed through your work-based reflective learning?
- How will this benefit the children, families and staff you work with and the setting, school, service you work in?
- How will you disseminate new theories in professional practice?

Reflective threads

How have the following three reflective threads within the spiral of reflection informed your reflective learning?

Employment experience

- What is your work history, experience and current employment?
- How has this informed your reflection?

Vocational and theoretical reflection

- Who has influenced your thinking through reading academic literature and research?
- What has influenced your thinking through visits or other sources for reflection?

Reflective conversations

- Who have you talked to?
- How have they challenged your thinking?
- How have they strengthened your knowledge and understanding?
- How have they enabled your self-confidence and articulation about provision and practice?

> *Work-based reflective learning*
>
> Consider how the Model of Work-based Reflective Learning has helped you reflect upon your practice.
>
> - What have you learnt about your professional practice?
> - What have you learnt about yourself as a reflective early years practitioner?

 ## Summary

The chapter has examined work-based learning within higher education. The close relationship between work-based learning and reflective practice has been explored. The concept of work-based reflective learning is introduced through a model of reflective change. Through case studies, the contribution of work-based reflective learning as a process for change in provision and practice has been demonstrated. The transformational contribution of work-based reflective learning for practitioners' professional learning and development has been discussed, demonstrated by examples of reflective learning within work contexts. Reflective questions have given opportunity for engagement in the model of work-based reflective learning.

In the next chapter, the contribution of Work-based Reflective Learning upon practitioners' vocational development is explored.

Further reading

This comprehensive book discusses many aspects of workplace learning:
Malloch, M., Cairns, L., Evans, K. and O'Conner, B.N. (eds) (2011) *The Sage Handbook of Workplace Learning*. London: Sage.

This book provides examples of work-based learning within a range of early years contexts:
Rawlings, A. (2008) *Studying Early Years: A Guide to Work-based Learning*. Maidenhead: Open University Press.

4

Reflective Vocational Progression

Chapter overview

Work-based reflective learning is further explored in this chapter demonstrating its contribution to practitioners' professional progression, employment opportunities and their vocational work with children and families through five themes: professional vocational practice; academic knowledge and professional knowledge; enhanced employability; lifelong learning and progression; and work-based research and practice. The themes are illuminated by reflective practitioners' voices and case studies. There is opportunity to reflect upon your vocational progression.

This chapter will:
- Explore the contribution of work-based reflective learning for practitioners' vocational work with children and families.
- Discuss the contribution of work-based reflective learning for the development of practitioners' specialized knowledge, personal and professional learning, employment opportunities and vocational progression.
- Demonstrate vocational progression with examples from practitioners' professional practice.

Vocational learning

The terms 'vocational learning' and 'academic learning' reflect the nature of learning in further and higher education. Traditionally, undergraduate degree courses have focused upon the acquisition of knowledge through subject-based learning by engaging in academic literature and research, predominantly conducted in the lecture theatre, seminar room and library. Prior to the Industrial Revolution all vocational learning was undertaken on the job and within the work-place, then formal education and training opportunities such as apprenticeships were introduced (Hager, 2011). The notion of vocational preparation for employment and working in the professions, such as teacher training, contributes to identity formation and is part of vocational education (Hager, 2011). Vocationally focused courses, such as teaching, social work and childcare courses, are delivered in further education colleges, universities and training organizations. Vocational learning values work as a site of learning for work and a source of curriculum knowledge (Solomon and Boud, 2011), pedagogy which challenges conventional higher education thinking and practice (Evans et al., 2011).

There is anecdotal evidence of a divide between vocational and academic qualifications beginning with secondary education; often childcare or media courses are regarded as of less value than academic subjects such as mathematics and science. This view can continue into further and higher education through the course, subject and type of degree chosen; for example, should I study childcare or A levels at further education college? Should I take science, early childhood studies or media studies at university? Should my award be a foundation, ordinary or honours degree?

Foundation degrees straddle the divide between vocational and academic learning and further and higher education sectors. The central work-based learning element of FDs integrate vocational learning with academic learning. The contribution of employers in the design and delivery of FDs links the award closely with employment (QAA, 2004). Hager (2011) regards workplace learning as multi-layered, concerning individual and organizational learning and change, adult learning, relationships, meaning-making and identity formation. Similarly, work-based reflective learning concerns transformational learning and change for early years practitioners' personal and professional development. The following five themes:

- professional vocational learning
- academic knowledge and understanding
- enhanced employability
- lifelong learning and progression
- work-based research and practice

demonstrate the contribution of work-based reflective learning for early years practitioners' personal and professional development, and vocational progression in the FD case study.

Professional vocational practice

Practitioners' daily work activity provides meaningful contexts for learning to take place and for their professional practice to be valued. Work-based learning is embedded within a philosophy of reflective learning and practice (Costley, 2011). The work context provides opportunity for practitioners to question and think about their practice and identify areas for improvement. Through college- and university-based teaching, independent reading and study, students and practitioners learn about early years influences, knowledge, theories and theorists, providing new and developed knowledge to reflect upon and understand practice. Work-based learning brings practice into learning, and reflection helps practitioners to fit theory with practice. Reflective practice extends professional practice through questioning and challenge, and contextual learning and engagement with real-life activities complement academic learning (Lakes, 2011), which supports career development and professional identity formation. It is through critical reflection that capability within the professional practice context develops (Costley, 2011), as this FD graduate's reflection shows.

Reflective practitioner's voice

I liked the work-based learning as it brings your practice into learning. I have become more reflective. Reflective practice implements everything I do. I understand why reflection is important, to improve your practice, and what it is to be reflective. I know what is right for children but reflection makes you think 'why' and the theory backs up what you did and you generally reflect about your practice.

The following case study is an example of a practitioner reflecting upon her practice through newly gained knowledge.

 Case study: *Reflective thinking*

Maryan is a playgroup leader working with a small group of children in a threading bead activity, counting beads with the children as they threaded them onto a cord. During her FD studies she read about children's

(Continued)

(Continued)

mathematical learning and development through the writing of Linda Pound, and about children's creative learning and development through the writing of Bernadette Duffy. She uses her newly found knowledge to reflect upon the maths activity she is doing with the children, appreciating that through the counting activity she can develop children's language and creative skills by asking open-ended questions to further their thinking about mathematical ordering, sorting, patterns, sequencing and colours.

The knowledge Maryan had gained through her professional learning had enabled her to view her work differently. The following questions will help you to reflect upon your work with children.

 Questions for reflection: *Reflecting on knowledge*

- Is there a writer who has influenced your understanding of children's learning and development?
- If so, how has this informed your practice?
- How have you modified your practice in light of this knowledge?

Academic and professional knowledge

Early years practitioners' underpinning knowledge helps inform their everyday practice with young children, families, agencies and practitioners they work with (Nutbrown and Page, 2008). There are a large number of practitioners working in the early years who have substantial experience of working in the sector individually and collectively. This experience of practice should provide a rich resource to inform professional knowledge and practice. However, some practitioners routinely carry out activities with children yet are unable to talk about why they do these activities or to link theory to their professional practice (Penn, 2008).

Students and practitioners studying at higher education level engage with theories, theorists, research and writers in the field of Early Childhood, informing their understanding of practice, providing opportunity to reconstruct their pedagogic practices through reflecting upon academic and professional knowledge. Early years practitioners form a pedagogical base of values, beliefs and principles of practice evolved from experience of practice, academic and professional knowledge and reflection. The way practitioners understand, interpret and construct Early Childhood and government policy is linked to their values and beliefs, knowledge and experience and the context of practice in which they work (Penn, 2008). Through continuous reflection of their pedagogy and beliefs, practitioners become 'agents of change' within the setting, school or service in which they work (Peeters and Vandenbroeck, 2011).

The Effective Provision of Pre-school Education (EPPE) study (Sylva et al., 2010) indicated that a highly qualified workforce contributes to the quality of pre-school provision. Qualified teachers contribute to children's learning outcomes when they lead the pedagogical practice of others (Owen and Haynes, 2008). The EPPE study has influenced government policy in developing a graduate-led early years workforce (DfES, 2005) of highly qualified graduate leaders with academic and professional knowledge to lead pedagogical practice and integrated provision.

During the past 20 years the development of a respected body of academic and professional knowledge for Early Childhood has emerged through the development of undergraduate degrees. The introduction of Early Childhood Studies degrees in the 1990s as a specialist subject area in universities and the professional award of nationally recognized Early Years Sector-Endorsed Foundation Degrees in 2001 provided a field of academic and professional knowledge for early years practitioners' developing professional roles and responsibilities (Calder, 2008).

The Common Core of Skills and Knowledge (CCSK) (CWDC, 2010a) describes the basic skills and knowledge required for those working with children and young people in an integrated way. The CCSK comprises six areas of skills and knowledge for the children and young people's workforce: effective communication and engagement with children, young people and families; child and person development; safeguarding and promoting the welfare of children and young people; supporting transitions; multi-agency working and integrated working; and information sharing. These core skills and knowledge are identified by those who work within the early years, primary, secondary and youth service as vocationally relevant (CWDC, 2010).

The development of knowledge and skills relevant for employment is a feature of FDs (Jones, 2008), and the CCSK is included in the curriculum of current nationally recognized Sector-Endorsed Early Years Foundation Degrees (SEYFD). The integration of work-based learning with academic knowledge (QAA, 2004) provides pedagogy for the development of professional skills and knowledge within the work context. Graduate practitioners in the FD case study gained specialized knowledge about the early years, including children's learning and development and working with families. Through their specialized academic and professional knowledge their confidence as professionals developed, and they were able to articulate their values and beliefs to other professionals, as this reflective comment shows.

Reflective practitioner's voice

I've increased my knowledge, I feel I have specialized knowledge in the early years and I can talk about the subject. The Head Teacher had been to a conference about babies' brain development and we discussed it together, she felt she could discuss it with me because of my knowledge of child development.

Similarly, Jones (2008) and Lumsden (2008) found students studying EYSEFDs recognized that they had become more reflective and confident practitioners. Their self-confidence and self-esteem had increased as their professional practice and knowledge were valued by others. Due to the FD graduates' increased academic and professional knowledge they are viewed by others differently, valued and included more in the work of the setting. The development of vocational learning and practice was empowering, providing practitioners with agency to change and improve their own practice and influence others in their work place (Jones, 2008). This reflective practitioner shares her new-found knowledge in supporting and mentoring others.

Reflective practitioner's voice

Now I've got the foundation degree my approach to work is different. I've taken on mentoring others. I'm mentoring a foundation degree student and two NVQs and one in their initial childcare training.

Enhanced employability

The relationship between academic knowledge, professional learning and practice contributes to practitioners' employability. All knowledge has a context through which it was originally developed and for knowledge to be used in another context it has to be recontextualized for integration into new contexts of practice (Evans et al., 2011). Foundation degrees provide opportunities for vocational progression that is academically rigorous and employment related (Longhurst, 2006), and is strongly orientated to employability skills and specialist knowledge (Heist, 2005). The development of transferable skills of communication, information technology and interpersonal skills is also important in the increasingly competitive employment climate. The collaboration of employers and programme providers in the design and delivery of foundation degrees ensures relevance in curriculum content to equip learners with the skills and knowledge relevant to their employment, so satisfying the requirements of employees and employers (QAA, 2004).

To secure change in employment, practitioners have to demonstrate that they have developed 'vocational practice', a mix of knowledge and skills that meets employers' needs and the current work context (Guile, 2011). This was evident in the FD case study, a significant number of graduate practitioners had been promoted in their work setting, or gained new employment during or at the completion of their FD studies. This graduate reflects upon her new employment:

Reflective practitioner's voice

I wouldn't have got the job without the foundation degree as it was a requirement to have a degree or an equivalent. Doing a degree vocationally was a different way of evidencing knowledge and experience in depth.

Through gaining higher education qualifications new employment opportunities opened up for practitioners within and beyond their setting, with change in responsibilities, however not always with increased financial remuneration. Through their studies some FD graduates had redefined themselves as professionals and used their qualification for career progression beyond their existing work setting. The FD award provided a catalyst and opportunity for progression, as this FD graduate's comment shows:

Reflective practitioner's voice

It's not about the qualification but it's about what you do with it. The foundation degree is the rope to pull you up but you've got to climb the rope yourself.

Lifelong learning and career progression

Lifelong learning concerns access to education from birth and throughout life (Harris and Chrisholm, 2011). The learning dispositions for continuous education, professional learning and development and establishing a career for learning begin early in life. Lifelong learning is supported by the concept of widening participation, providing learning and training opportunities for those who have largely been excluded from educational opportunity, particularly at higher education level. Higher education should not be regarded as one experience in a person's lifetime but a continuum of learning where people can be expected to move in and out of education throughout their lives (Longhurst, 2006). The FD award is central to this approach, a stand-alone award of 240 credits which can be built upon with a 'top-up' stage for progression to an ordinary or honours degree, providing opportunities for lifelong learning and career progression.

Foundation degrees have enhanced educational opportunities for those who did not pursue further education when leaving school (Lumsden, 2008). Early years FDs have provided higher educational opportunity, particularly for women who left secondary education with few formal qualifications, and raised aspirations for this gendered workforce, many of whom have progressed further in academic and professional qualifications and careers. The development of personal and professional confidence has motivated practitioners to further their careers. A FD graduate reflects upon the impact of her award upon her lifelong learning and career progression:

Reflective practitioner's voice

The foundation degree gives you the belief, 'I can do it', I always thought I never could study but it gives you confidence and the belief 'I can do it'. I didn't have the belief I could do the BA or anything. The opportunity came at the right time. I wanted something to challenge me. It helped me on the professional ladder. I've gone up the ladder of qualifications. I've done the FD, the BA and the GTTP teacher training then I will be complete. The foundation degree has been a huge stepping stone, a door opened to progress further.

Students undertaking research in their work setting as part of their higher educational learning have gained in-depth knowledge and understanding of the early years and professional confidence. Work-based mentors in the FD case study valued the graduates' work-based research projects and the impact upon provision and practice that their research had made.

Work-based research and practice

Research has many layers of meaning and application, ranging from collecting facts, locating detailed information, planning activity, checking information by paper, electronic or human sources, to conducting a research project as part of an undergraduate or postgraduate degree. The work context of an early years setting, school or children's service provides an opportunity to 'research reality' through investigating real issues about provision and practice (Penn, 2008: 21). Through findings researchers make recommendations to develop and modify service provision, pedagogy and professional practice individually as a practitioner or, at an organizational level. The notion of 'work-based research' is located within practitioners' work practices; the research question(s) for investigation emerge from their work context and everyday activity with children and families. In an environment informed by work-based reflective learning, practitioners work in a climate of reflective change and improvement. The ability for self-reflection is central to practitioner research (Rawlings, 2008) and work-based learning. Reflective questions around the words *why*, *what*, *how* and *where* form a structure to investigate provision and practice, test theory, review government policy, and construct meaning and understanding with others for individual or organizational change.

Work-based research links practice with theory in a meaningful way. Penn (2008: 22) highlights 'theories are at the heart of practice', however, in researching a work-based issue, the investigation does not have to begin with reading about theory from academic books as this can obscure new insights into practice and service provision. The Model of Work-based Reflective Learning in Chapter 3 demonstrates the development of new theories of professional practice through a reflective cycle of change. By sharing new-found meaning and knowledge with others, work-based research influences practice (Rawlings, 2008). The reflexive relationships between research and practice show the contexts of work and learning impact on the development of practice (Malloch et al., 2011), particularly in action research where reflection plays a central role in the action cycle of change (Roberts-Holmes, 2011).

In researching an early years topic or issue, different perspectives bring a range of views, providing a lens for analysis and construction of meaning. The views may be from parents, children, practitioners or other professionals, coming from multiple sources provides validation and verification of facts, moving the investigation from 'I think this' to 'this is what others think' (Rawlings, 2008). A work-based research project should be planned and designed thoughtfully, incorporating research methodology and research ethics acknowledging individual rights through informed consent and confidentiality. Many early years work-based research projects are case studies, action research or use the mosaic approach in researching children's perspectives, enabling children's voices to be heard, and acknowledging their rights in a respectful way (Clark, 2004).

 An example of a research project with children using the mosaic approach is included as a case study in Chapter 10.

Early years practitioners acquire a high level of observational skills through their nursery nurse and childcare training. They routinely observe children in their daily practice, informing their understanding of children's social, emotional, cognitive and physical development. Observation is a way of recording, seeing patterns, making comparisons, connections and judgements through considered reflection and analysis. Observation is valuable as a research tool. Through reflection and analysis, observations can reveal unknown aspects of a child's development, provision or practice. The following case study shows the contribution of observation within reflective learning.

 Case Study: *Superhero play*

Neelab works in private day care as an early years practitioner. Her research project concerns how media and popular culture surrounding children influences their play and behaviour. Observation is one of her research methods.

Reflection and analysis

I first observed Reeve, a 3-year-old boy, one morning engaged in superhero play with one of his friends, Alex, also a 3-year-old boy. Throughout this observation, it was apparent there was a shared interest between the boys in the cartoon characters of Scooby-Doo and Ben-10 they had seen on television programmes and in comics they read. Their shared focus contributed to their interactions with each other; they were highly motivated and put a lot of effort and enthusiasm into the activity, being deeply involved in their play scenario. Their play began with negotiating the character roles; Alex wanted to be a particular character, but Reeve insisted 'no . . . me Humungousaur!' Alex accepted Reeve's perspective and that he was now this particular character. There were some clear imitative actions and phrases that were drawn from the television programmes which Reeve used to represent his ideas through his play.

Reeve was forming friendships through superhero play. I discussed this with his mother who informed me that Reeve and his older brother engaged in superhero play regularly at home. By using this form of role play, he is able to represent his ideas physically and through language. He plays confidently through his own interests from the media and popular culture he is surrounded by, bridging the gap between the home and the setting.

Throughout their play, both boys engaged in weapon play, using construction toys such as Lego to construct replica guns and swords, using them in their play with associated noises. Weapon play is a topic the nursery team has discussed on previous occasions, debating whether it is appropriate to allow weapon play or not. We put it on the staff meeting's agenda, allowing time for staff to reflect upon the issues of superhero and gun play, developing a nursery policy for practice. Some staff felt that children see enough violence on the television without engaging in it at nursery. By reflecting upon Reeve's interest in superhero and gun play, I am aware of Holland's (2003) view to look beyond the weapon to the child holding it. In Reeve's play, his stick became a gun, then a sword and back again to a gun. Reeve's imagined character was also transformed from Scooby-Doo to Ben-10 to Humungousaur. As Reeve's ideas are transformed his thinking is changing and being clarified. By imagining the stick is no longer a stick, Reeve is giving new meanings and representation in his play.

Throughout my observations, I have noted that Alex always brings in several superhero figures from home which, if he is not holding, are always near to him. On reflection, this is more than just an interest in the character figures he brings but are transitional objects representing the security of home. I noticed that once his key worker showed an interest in these figures, he settled away from his mother into the nursery with little upset. Alex used the security of these transitional objects to explore different modes of representation, such as creative, imaginative and physical, with a feeling of safety.

Recommendations for practice

However, through discussion and reflecting upon pertinent issues, we came to the conclusion that we did not want to stifle children's imagination. We decided to explain to the children that they need to be kind and respectful to each other during their play. We agreed that we would intercede if the children put themselves or others in danger but were not to intervene if children construct guns or similar weapons from any of the resources in the nursery.

As a staff we reflected upon a 'child's world' in the twenty-first century; their home and local environment is full of media and popular culture which we don't value as a resource for learning in the nursery. A child who brings a soft toy, plastic figure, DVD or game to nursery is asked to put it in a box until home time. Through reflective discussion and reading about Jackie Marsh's work of using the Teletubbies television characters to inspire young children's literacy development (Marsh, 1999), practitioners are now going to use the toys and books children bring to the nursery in activities, valuing them as resources for learning and in helping children's transition from home to nursery.

The case study shows the value of observation as a tool for reflective research. The following questions will help you think about your observational work.

 Questions for reflection: *Reflective observation*

Consider an observation you have carried out, reflect upon the information you recorded.

- Did the information reveal anything new?
- Did knowledge from other observations, reading books or discussion with other practitioners inform your analysis?
- How did the observation analysis inform your provision and practice?

 Summary

This chapter has further examined work-based reflective learning, its contribution to practitioners' professional progression, employment opportunities and their vocational work with children and families. The themes of professional vocational practice; academic knowledge and professional knowledge; enhanced employability; lifelong learning and progression; work-based research and practice demonstrated the impact of work-based reflective learning for practitioners' vocational progression. Throughout the chapter the themes were illustrated by examples of practitioners' progression and case studies from professional practice. Reflective questions enabled reflection upon these themes.

The next chapter considers work-based reflective learning as pedagogy in higher education.

Further reading

There is a case study of an EYSEFD in Chapter 10 of:
Miller, L. and Cable, C. (2008) *Professionalism in the Early Years*. London: Hodder and Stoughton.

There are examples of professional practice from international contexts in Chapter 9 of:
Penn, H. (2008) *Understanding Early Childhood: Issues and Controversies*. 2nd edn. Maidenhead: Open University Press.

5

Work-based Reflective Pedagogy

Chapter overview

Work-based Reflective Learning, teaching and assessment pedagogy enables and enhances the development of practitioners' professional development within their work setting. Work-based reflective learning as pedagogy for vocational continuing professional development in higher education is examined. The concept of 'wrap-around learning' provides a model for flexible study and access to higher education. Reflective practitioners' voices and a case study provide examples of professional learning through reflective pedagogy. There is opportunity to consider your continuous professional learning through reflective questions.

This chapter will:
- Discuss a reflective approach to transformational continuous professional learning.
- Examine work-based reflective pedagogy in curriculum design, teaching, learning and assessment.
- Explore the concept of lifelong learning and widening participation.
- Explore flexible student-centred study through the concept of 'wrap-around learning' to facilitate access to higher education.
- Provide opportunities for personal and professional reflection.

Continuing professional learning and development

The workforce who work in a school, setting or service are the most important resource and key to children's learning and development and the success of the organization. Continuing professional development (CPD) is a term used for ongoing education and training for professionals who are expected to continue learning throughout their career (Bubb and Earley, 2007). There is an expectation for those working in the early years to be committed to their own professional learning. In the climate of changing government policy, it is important for teachers and practitioners to be up to date with current policy, practice and research to further their qualifications and career opportunities.

Professional development activities should enhance the knowledge and skills of practitioners and teachers. There are a variety of informal and formal activities for professional learning, for example, short- and long-term courses, school- and setting-based projects, network meetings, workshops, conferences, mentoring, coaching, visits to settings, schools or children's services and secondment. Bolam (1993: 3) identifies types of CPD activity by three categories:

- Professional training, emphasizing practical information.
- Professional education, emphasizing theory and research-based knowledge.
- Professional support, aiming to develop job experience and performance.

Continuing professional development activities are carried out individually and with others, enabling practitioners and teachers to think about their practice, improve ways of working for the benefit of children's learning and development and enhance their knowledge and skills, their personal and professional growth, self-confidence and job satisfaction (Bubb and Earley, 2007). The Teaching Development Agency (TDA, 2008) identifies the value of reflective activity within the process of continuing professional learning for developing an individual's professional attributes, knowledge, understanding and skills. Opportunities for reflection support individuals' professional needs and improve their practice. The chapter now discusses opportunities for reflective continuous professional learning within curriculum design, content and pedagogy of higher education programmes.

Higher level work-based reflective learning

Work-based learning as a mode of learning is taught and assessed in higher education in many ways. The most effective way is when work-based learning is embedded within a programme's curriculum, teaching and assessment strategy, rather than 'bolted on' to a subject-based programme, as students are able to construct meaning, theory and develop reflective practice through a work-based curriculum and

pedagogy (Challis, 2006). Work-based assessment in higher education is more than recording skills and competences; work-based
methods of assessment require theoretical underpinning knowledge
enabling students to think at a higher level about practice. As they
are familiar with and understand the context in which they work,
practitioners and teachers are able to formulate questions about their
work contexts and their role within them, offer interventions into
practices they have researched, analysed, critiqued and theorized.

Reflection encourages deeper understanding of actions and more
sustainable learning that can lead to improvement in professional
practice and provide the learner with abilities and skills to engage
with their own learning and development (Beaney, 2004; Paige-Smith
and Craft, 2011). Effective practitioners are reflective people with a
sense of agency who become change-makers within their work contexts and more widely within their professional field (Costley and
Armsby, 2007). Through reflective practice, practitioners have the
potential to transform what they do and what children and families
experience (Paige-Smith and Craft, 2011) and become enquiring professionals (Anning and Edwards, 2003). Reflective learning is agency
for professional change and transformation.

Work-based reflective pedagogy

The work-based reflective pedagogy within the FD case study and its
contribution to practitioners' professional learning is now explored.
The reflective teaching and learning pedagogy within the FD curriculum supported one of the programme aims in encouraging students
to become reflective practitioners within their work setting. The
structure of the teaching and assessment strategy enabled students to
critically reflect upon current provision and practice, and anticipated
development in education and care. The design of the curriculum, the
teaching and assessment strategy enabled students to reflect upon
their practice, connect theory to their practice, so furthering their
understanding, and develop new knowledge and ways of thinking by
generating 'theories in use' (Moon, 2006: 7). The reflective pedagogy
in which work-based learning and reflection was embedded within
each module's learning outcomes (Challis, 2006) provided a reflective
thread throughout the FD curriculum. One learning outcome in each
module asked students to reflect upon and modify their practice in
light of current research, academic literature and their professional
learning. An FD graduate reflects upon the reflective aspect of the
modules studied:

Reflective practitioner's voice

The whole process of the foundation degree is reflective, every module made me reflect upon what I can do. It was how the modules were written around practice. In the learning outcomes, it was where the reading linked to practice for the practitioner. Every module had a section on reflective practice. It made you look at things in a different way. It made you think why should I do it? Before, I just did things, the reading and the research opened my eyes and I saw different ways of doing things and this helped me reflect where I was in the context of what I provided for children.

The module about special educational needs aimed to develop knowledge and understanding of approaches for working with children with special educational needs (SEN). The assessment required students to critically analyse a case study of a child and evaluate provision for the inclusion of the child within the school or setting. The following case study shows how provision within the work setting provides a context for reflective evaluation.

 Case Study: *Inclusive education*

Danuta works in a nursery, she is the key person to Oliver, supporting his additional needs and working closely with his family, multi-agencies and professionals. Oliver is 20 months old. Shortly after birth he was diagnosed with cerebral palsy. There are several professionals in the multi-agency team involved in Oliver's care, including his key person, health visitor, speech and language therapist, physiotherapist, pediatric registrar and a general practitioner.

There are clear processes and procedures in the nursery regarding provision for children with special educational needs. We have a special educational needs co-ordinator (SENCO) who oversees all the children in the nursery, assessing those with additional need. It is her role to offer support and co-ordinate bi-monthly review meetings to discuss individual children's needs and follow up identified actions. A meeting was held in which all agencies, nursery staff and parents met to review Oliver's progress. We were made aware of Oliver's diagnosis by his health visitor who is the lead professional supporting Oliver and his family, co-ordinating various professionals and agencies involved in Oliver's care, and acting as a point of contact for them.

The meeting was held in the Parents Room at the nursery. We believe that partnership working with parents and carers is important; it can have a positive impact on a child's learning and development. With this in mind, the SENCO gathered information about the intervention identified in his

Individual Education Plan (IEP) for Oliver's mother to get a holistic view of her son to enable us to plan effectively. The IEP was developed by the SENCO with Oliver's key person and physiotherapist. There are targets for developmental progress identified. The review meeting is an opportunity to reflect upon Oliver's progress, by reviewing and modifying his intervention and progress targets. The various professionals bring a different perspective to Oliver's progress and development, enabling many views to be reflected upon.

The use of observations is central to the IEP process. Oliver is regularly observed by his key person, who recognizes his interests, and his physiotherapist, who understands his physical well-being. Their observation and evaluation of progress inform his IEP targets. Through observing Oliver, I discovered he particularly enjoys singing and playing musical instruments. I mentioned this at the review meeting; a target specific to this interest was included in the review of his IEP, to develop his hand–eye co-ordination during music time by encouraging him to hold a shaker or bells in each hand or to encourage him to bang on a drum with both hands. Oliver's mother also enjoys music and she would be able to help with this target at home by borrowing the shakers from the nursery to use with Oliver.

The case study was part of an essay in Danuta's FD assessment, enabling her to reflect upon her practice and professionally learn from it. The following questions will enable you to reflect upon an aspect of your professional learning and the impact upon your work context.

 Questions for reflection: *Reflecting upon your professional learning*

Consider a professional learning event you have attended, this may be a CPD course, a workshop or a network meeting, a visit to a setting, school or children's centre, or one of the sessions of a college or university course you are attending. The questions will help you consider the impact of this event upon your professional learning, provision and practice.

- What did you learn?

Identify at least one significant component of the event; this may be some new knowledge, a new book, author, research paper, report; some aspect of practice you were shown, read about or someone you met.

- How has it influenced your thinking?
- How has it made you view your practice differently?
- How has it influenced your practice?

The case study above demonstrates FDs as a higher education award are 'profoundly learner focused' (Longhurst, 2006:7). The curriculum design needs to be informed by this principle; the programme aims and learning outcomes should focus upon the student as a learner and a practitioner within the work environment. Work-based reflective learning draws upon the work environment by integrating opportunities for critical evaluation, analysis and reflective thinking within the work context. It recognizes what is being learnt through employment and within the workplace, creating a framework for professional learning, development and improvement of practice (Longhurst, 2006). Reflective practice is a way for transformation and change, a process through which practitioners can discover what they understand, how they work through self-awareness and a way of discovering new and better ways of doing things (Osterman and Kottamp, 1993). Writing is an effective way to develop self-awareness and reflective practice.

Approaches to reflective writing in higher education degrees are now discussed.

Reflective writing

Undergraduate degrees are usually assessed through coursework and written assignments, predominantly essays. The FD case study had a diverse range of assessment modes in work-based assessment activities, allowing flexibility to accommodate differing work settings, roles and responsibilities. The work-based activities included reflective assessment tasks: designing an information leaflet for parents; carrying out a SWOT analysis of provision, identifying areas of strength, weakness, opportunity and threats; observation analysis; reflective summaries; research project; presentations; posters; report writing; case studies; and action planning. The topic for each assessment emerged from within the students' work settings and their everyday practice.

The literacy-based assessment mode valued the process of writing as an important aspect of reflection. Plummer (2001: 46) regards 'writing for reflective practice as a first-order activity in the reflective mode, it no longer "captures" reality but helps to "construct" it.' The range of writing modes in the FD case study enabled each student to focus clearly upon their personal and professional development (Bolton, 2010). The expression of reflection can be an area of difficulty for some students; they may have reflective skills but not reflective writing skills (Rutter, 2006). The representation of reflective learning is an area of learning in itself for, unless students are able to express themselves in a reflective way, their reflection will not be recognized (Moon, 2006).

Through reflective writing, students should be able to articulate their everyday contextualized practice. Reflective writing is a personal experience enabling students to express their work-based experience and develop their own working theories and apply this to their professional practice (Bolton, 2010). Through critical reflection within the writing process, professional expertise is developed (Schon, 1987). Reflective writing draws upon deep experience, and creates close contact with emotions, thoughts and experiences particularly in journal writing, which is a personal expression of experience and as 'dynamic as speech' (Bolton, 2005: 48). The use of a reflective journal helps reflective study. The FD graduates' 'reflective learning journeys' (Chapter 9) demonstrate the powerful pedagogy of autobiographical reflective writing in professional learning.

 The use of a reflective journal for developing reflective study is further discussed in Chapter 6.

 There are examples of reflective writing in graduate practitioners' 'Reflective learning journeys' in Chapter 9 and in their 'Continuing learning pathways' in Chapter 10.

There can be a division between reflective writing used in work-based FDs and the academic writing used in traditionally academic BA degrees. Graduates in the FD case study found a problematic transition to the 'top-up' final stage of undergraduate BA (Hons) degrees at their home university. The students' vocationally based reflective writing was not valued and respected in the BA assessment as it had been in their FD assessment, some students receiving lower grades when they used reflective writing in their BA essays. This FD graduate reflects upon the differing pedagogy of the degree programmes and the impact upon the expected writing styles.

Reflective practitioner's voice

I am completing my 'top-up' stage three on the BA Early Childhood Studies. On that course you read books and then apply to practice. On the foundation

(Continued)

(Continued)

degree it turns back on its head, you start with your practice and then read the books. The foundation degree is work-based, it combines academic with practice. The foundation degree is real; it makes you confident as a practitioner, before you explore other academic people. We deal with people and children and can apply theory to real situations rather than hypothetical ones. Specialized knowledge is your practice and it's in looking after children, not reading books of knowledge as you have knowledge of real children. You question experts in books based on your knowledge of children and practice. As my foundation degree studies developed, I looked at children and then read the books about what the experts said. Making sense of theories made me develop a real argument for my practice.

On the BA you approach assignments in a different way and write in a different way. You can do the BA in isolation from children and not link to practice. On the foundation degree you need to be in practice as it is more reflective than the BA. There should be a BA foundation degree.

Transition and progression

The two differing teaching, learning and assessment pedagogies of 'vocational' (practical and applied) and 'academic' (theoretical and conceptual) (Beaney, 2006: 2) can produce division between vocationally focused FDs and academically focused BA degrees and inequality of status, although the first and second stages of both types of degrees are credited with the same number of higher education credits (240). Both vocational and academic writing styles are of equal value in developing intellectual knowledge and understanding. Work-based reflective practice concerns improving practice and generating theories to understand that improvement, such 'real-world knowledge' (Roberts-Holmes, 2011: 7) produced by early childhood practitioners, is as good as that within the established academic community. However, to ensure the vocationally based real-world knowledge has validity, it should involve critical reflection and systematic enquiry through engagement with academic knowledge and research.

The FD graduate reflectively comments above, that there should be a 'BA foundation degree', highlighting the need for transition and progression between the two pedagogies of work-based reflective learning and academic learning, particularly relevant in the development of early years graduates, many of whom progress as FD graduates to BA Early Years, Early Childhood and Education programmes. Work-based learning is 'a potentially powerful pedagogy which is capable of transforming not only learning at and from work but also influencing more traditional forms of provision' (Foundation Degree Forward, 2005: 1). There is an emerging recognition for a teaching, learning and assessment pedagogy that builds upon and develops work-based learning pedagogy found in FDs in a critical reflective pedagogy, developing work-based learning to a new level for ordinary and honours degree study, and providing pedagogy to smooth transition and progression in vocational learning and academic study.

Lifelong learning and widening participation

Lifelong learning concerns the concept of learning as a process throughout an individual's life, from the cradle to the grave. Foundation degrees intend to make a valuable contribution to lifelong learning through one of the defining characteristics of 'articulation and progression' (QAA, 2004: 5). Clear routes that facilitate opportunities for successful progression from FDs to other awards are an important feature of FDs and a requirement for the validation of a programme.

The National Research Study of the Early Years Sector-Endorsed Foundation Degree found that for some FD graduates, especially those who had not studied for some time, the course had sharpened their desire for study (Knight et al., 2006), and course completers were strongly motivated and interested in enhancing their qualifications and progressing within the early years and childcare sectors (Snape et al., 2007). Foundation degree graduates should be able to utilize opportunities for lifelong learning (QAA, 2004).

Early years FDs enabled practitioners to access the concept of a 'climbing frame of qualifications in the training of childcare workers' developed by Abbott and Hevey (2001) informing the development of the Qualifications and Credit Framework (QCF) (CWDC, 2010b), a system for recognizing skills and qualifications by awarding credit for qualifications and units of learning. Since the EYSEFD research (2006; 2007) many FD graduates have climbed the rope to further qualifications, BA ordinary and honours degrees, and nationally recognized professional awards (EYPS, HLTA) and have progressed in their employment.

 This progression is further discussed in Chapters 9 and 10.

The following FD graduate reflects upon the contribution of her FD studies to her continuing professional learning and vocational progression.

Reflective practitioner's voice

The foundation degree was a stepping stone to something else. Without this 'softer' introduction to higher education, I'm not sure I could have started, to come back into education and go straight to uni would be too much to handle and I know I would have backed out.

   The foundation degree helped me become a teacher. I did the SCIT Teacher Training programme (School Centred Initial Training). I am a qualified teacher and am doing a maternity leave now but I have got a permanent job in September teaching a Year 2 class. The foundation degree increased my employability. I have gone up the training ladder; the foundation degree was the first major step up the ladder.

Foundation degrees contribute to widening access to higher education, offering opportunities for those who otherwise would not have considered it an option (Heist, 2005) and aiming to improve opportunities for the existing workforce to 'earn and learn' (Longhurst, 2006: 4), appealing to social groups who are largely excluded from higher educational opportunity with few qualifications such as A levels, the recognized entry qualifications for higher education. The Labour Government (1997–2010) invested financially in the early years through supporting the training of the workforce. When the EYSEFD award was introduced in 2001, students were supported by a financial support package, and funding from the Transformation and Graduate Leader Funds (2006–11). Financial support from these funds made a significant difference to experienced women practitioners in particular, to access higher education, professional awards and graduate leadership training, previously financially inaccessible, providing widening access and participation in higher education, and supporting practitioners' capabilities for lifelong learning and career development.

 Further information about the financial support package can be found in the Introduction.

Through the financial support a more highly qualified workforce with increased personal and professional confidence and early years specialist knowledge (Lumsden, 2008) has emerged. Many experienced women practitioners studied part-time to accommodate work and family commitments. Flexible programme provision for this non-traditional group of students is now explored.

'Wrap-around learning': a flexible model for learning

Flexibility in study and programme provision is central to widening access and participation in higher education, flexibility is a defining characteristic of FDs (QAA, 2004). Many students studying Early Years and Early Childhood FD and BA degrees are non-traditional students, mature and experienced women practitioners, representative of the predominantly female early years workforce (Kay, 2005). Although higher education institutions have large numbers of mature female and male students, institutional practices within the organization, structure and pedagogy within higher education has not changed to accommodate, particularly, the needs of women students (Burke, 2006). There are many institutional structures existing between the office hours of 9 o'clock in the morning and 5 o'clock in the afternoon. These times are inconvenient for practitioners working in schools and early years settings and with childcare and family commitments. Consideration for flexible and accessible times outside normal working hours must be given to accommodate this growing group of non-traditional part-time students, many of whom are women. This could include times for students to enroll in the late evening or at weekends, to hand their assignments in a 'drop in box' outside working hours and during the weekend. Similarly, to be able to collect their assignment during the evening or at weekends. Students' basic needs for warmth, safety and food are important for students' learning. The facility for students to buy a hot meal and drink is important as many leave work and go straight to their class for study. After an evening or weekend class, the security of students should be considered; a well lit car park, the presence of security staff and a staffed reception, all provide a safe environment for students.

Women can face financial and familial barriers in returning to education (Wright, 2011). These include personal issues such as finance, transport, childcare, partner disapproval, becoming ill, caring for sick children or elderly parents; professional issues can include, an unexpected Ofsted inspection, an unsupportive manager or head, covering for absent staff, and lack of release from work. Women juggle many aspects of their lives, trying to integrate three areas: family, work and education. Wright (2011: 43) describes this as a 'triple triangle', which interlocks in the process of 'maintaining integrated lives'. Graduates in the FD case study were juggling complicated lives of family and work commitments, sometimes at the cost of their marriage and family; taking time out from their studies often meant they didn't return, as life somehow got in the way.

The women in the FD case study had to fit into a traditional part-time evening programme delivery, completing the award in three years, while fitting their family and work commitments into the programme schedule. Consideration was given to the characteristic of 'flexibility' in relation to the gender of the female student group. What were their study needs? And how are their gender needs made visible within higher education provision? How can the FD programme wrap around their family and employment needs? How can they have agency in their study? The development of a flexible programme delivery put the student at the centre of the learning process. The 'wrap-around learning' model for flexible learning is based around these questions.

- *What* modules do you want to study?
- *When* do you want to study?
- *Where* do you want to study?
- *When* do you want to graduate?

At the start of each year, each student develops an Individual Learning Plan with their personal tutor, fitting their study around their family and employment needs. Figure 5.1 illustrates the flexible provision wrapping around the student in a learner-centred way.

The elements and underpinning pedagogy for student-centred learning enabling flexible access to and participation in higher education, as shown in the Wrap-around Learning model, are now explained:

Flexible admission

- Advice, guidance and interviews are given throughout the year.
- Accredited Prior Experimental Learning (APEL) and Accredited Prior credit Learning (APcL) are used to fast track modules.

Flexible delivery times

- Two programme start dates (September, January) provide choice.
- The programme delivery is in the daytime, evening and on some Saturdays, giving choice of times to study.

Flexible choice of modules and study centres

- Students choose the number of modules to study.
- Students choose where to study. The programme is collaboratively delivered at the university, in three further education colleges and in two outreach centres. The different study locations make all the modules accessible to students throughout the year.
- Students plan their graduation date.

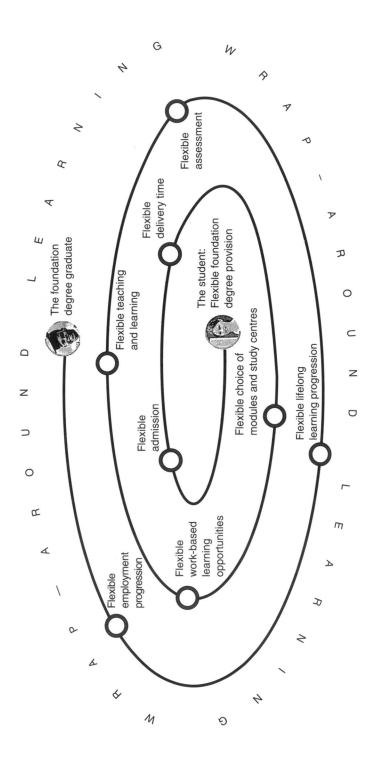

Figure 5.1 Wrap-around Learning: a flexible model for learning

Flexible work-based learning opportunities

- Learning outcomes are assessed within a negotiated work-based framework using each student's work context as the focus of assessment.
- Learning partnerships provide a three-way partnership dialogue between the tutor, student and work-based mentor for student review and providing relevant work-based learning opportunities.

Flexible teaching and learning

- Blended teaching and learning modes provide adaptable pedagogy for learning styles including e-learning, online resources, key lectures, directed reflective tasks, seminars, independent study, group tutorials, individual face-to-face, email and telephone tutorials, which also provide flexible times and ways for study.

Flexible assessment

- A diverse range of assessment modes suit different learning styles and assessment modes including essays, presentations, information leaflets, action plans, research projects and activity planning.

Flexible lifelong learning progression

- Students are able to progress to academic and professional awards, through taught, blended, distance and online learning modes.

Flexible employment progression

- The programme is collaboratively developed and regularly reviewed with employers, meeting workforce and sector needs.
- Practitioners working in the early years sector share their current practice with students in practitioner workshops during programme delivery.

An FD graduate reflects upon the flexible programme delivery and how it 'wrapped around' her personal and professional needs:

Reflective practitioner's voice

I did the foundation degree at the outreach centre which was the school where I worked. When I did it, I wouldn't have been allowed time to come to the university, but the university had the flexibility in the delivery and it allowed me to study while I worked and attend sessions where I worked. The foundation degree is learning while you work, meeting everyone's needs, building upon your practice, making learning accessible to practitioners. There was flexibility in how it was delivered; the choice of modules fitted your work needs or role.

> The delivery of the modules met the needs of the different practitioners in the group. If people live near a university they can go, if it's not on the doorstep it's difficult. The foundation degree being delivered in outreach centres is a massive bonus as it makes it accessible to people who can't get to the university.

The following questions will help you reflect upon your own flexible participation in higher education.

 Questions for reflection: *Flexible study*

Reflect upon the flexibility you have in your study.

- Are your study needs accommodated within your working and family life?
- How are your study needs flexibly 'wrapped around' your personal and professional needs?
- Do you have flexibility within your study time?
- Are their any barriers to you studying flexibly? If so, how can they be overcome?

 Summary

This chapter discussed a reflective approach to continuous professional learning through examining work-based reflective pedagogy and assessment in curriculum design, teaching, learning and assessment activity. Discussion about reflective writing highlighted the need for transition and progression in reflective vocational and academic pedagogy. The study needs of women practitioners were considered through a student-centred model of flexible learning which wraps around family and employment needs, providing agency in their study planning and learning. A case study and reflective practitioners' voices illustrated the themes explored.

The next chapter continues the discussion by exploring ways of becoming a reflective student.

Further reading

The value of writing in reflective learning is examined in this book:
Bolton, G. (2010) *Reflective Practice: Writing and Professional Development*. 3rd edn. London: Sage.

The author's integrated lives theory is explained in Chapter 4:
Wright, H. (2011) *Women Studying Childcare*. Stoke-on-Trent: Trentham Books.

Being a Reflective Student

Beginning study

Starting higher educational study concerns transition; from home to education, from school to college or university, from college to university. Transition is a time of change, through the process of transition an individual's position within their surrounding environment is altered (Bronfenbrenner, 1979), this may be a change in role, setting or both. The transition for students from the known to the unknown can be daunting. For many experienced practitioner students, it can be a long time since engagement in education, often since leaving school, and the transition from the safety of their home or workplace to a large university can be intimidating. For younger students also, the transition from the familiar school or college environment to a university too can seem daunting, transiting from supported to independent study and different expectations from lecturers rather than teachers whom they know. Students do overcome their fears and graduate with FD and BA degrees and, later, postgraduate MA degrees, with a sense of achievement, a change in personal and professional knowledge and confidence, as this FD graduate reflects:

Reflective practitioner's voice

Graduating with my foundation degree was the proudest day of my life. It was absolutely fantastic. I have a sense of achievement and pride.

For a student, the long-term goal is to achieve your degree and become a graduate, as this student did. There are many steps along the higher education pathway within the learning environment you have entered, whether the building you study in is a further education college, a university or an outreach centre such as a training centre or a hall in the local school. The following questions will help you at the start of your studies, along the pathway to being a reflective student.

 Questions for reflection: *Reflecting on transition to study*

During the first week of your programme, making a reflective time to consider the transition, and thinking about your hopes and fears, can help a smooth transition.

- What do I expect from the programme?
- What do I hope to achieve?
- What are my fears?
- Why do I have these fears?
- How will I approach the newness of the situation and alleviate my fears?
- Who will be able to help?

Starting to study

When beginning to study in higher education, it is important to regard yourself as 'a student' and to prioritize your study and learning as an important aspect within your life. The following areas will help you become an active student who will gain the most out of your studies (Hallet, 2004).

Creating study time

There will be many demands on your time: presentations to prepare; seminar papers to read; work-based activities to plan; essays to write; and assignment deadlines to meet. Study demands need to be integrated into other aspects of your life, such as family, social and work commitments, in a balanced way. Becoming a student means arranging your study life, being able to manage your time, to prioritize and to make effective use of time available. Key to becoming an efficient student is time management, prioritizing, taking control of your study time. The following reflective activity will help you think about how you spend your time and then how best to use your time for studying.

> ## 〰️ Questions for reflection: *Managing my time*
>
> Consider a typical week you have and identify how you spend your time. For each day block out the unavailable time you have using these descriptions of time.
>
> - *Committed time* – this is time you have commitments and arrangements that cannot be altered; this may be childcare, travelling time, time spent at work, regular social commitments or meetings.
> - *Maintenance time* – this is time spent to support your life, in shopping, cooking, eating meals, cleaning and sleeping.
> - *Adaptable time* – this is time you have available to arrange study time.
>
> In your typical week, you will have identified some spaces of time available for you to study. Now consider when it is the best time for you to study, tick the most appropriate statements:
>
> - I need to work for at least two hours to achieve something.
> - I can only concentrate for two to three hours.

- I can think and study better in the morning.
- I can think and study better in the evening.
- I can think and study better at night time and very early morning.
- I can think and study better very early in the morning.
- I find it hard to work in the evenings after work.
- I find it better to study at weekends.
- I have to be at home to study.
- I prefer to study in the library.

Creating a place to study

It is important to create a special environment for you to study in; a place where you can leave things out such as books, notepads, pens and your personal computer. To tidy away after each study time only to set up again the next time, wastes time and energy, for example, changing a communal space as a dining table to an individual work station. It is much more productive to have a smaller designated area for your study space. Arranging a quiet time and space away from interruptions of the household is conducive to study. To prioritize this within the home with a notice on the door 'Do not disturb, student at work', or arranging for the children to be taken to the park for a few hours, will put your study into the household timetable.

Making a 'to do' list

The demands of study, assessment deadlines and requests from lecturers can be overwhelming, especially if more than one module is being studied at a time. For each module, the long-term goal is to write and pass the assignment. The required word limit of thousands of words can seem overwhelming, so it is helpful to break down the requirements for each assignment into smaller tasks; make a list of these shorter tasks, crossing them off when completed, gives a sense of achievement. If you have two hours for time to study, a short task on your list could be to read the first chapter in the course's core textbook for an essay topic and make notes. This is a more achievable task than to write your essay in the two hours you have. At the end of two hours you will be able to put a tick beside the task as achieved, motivating you to study more.

Being an active student

Students who engage in all programme activities develop and achieve more than those who do not. Being an active student means engaging in all opportunities: attending all the lectures, seminars and tutorials, making notes, asking questions, participating in the session's discussions, workshops, presentations, receiving feedback in a constructive way to modify and improve your work, this may be academic writing or work-based tasks, and regularly communicating with your personal tutor, lecturer and work-based mentor.

Having study support

It can be lonely studying in higher education, having a supportive friend as a study partner through your studies is helpful for sharing your studies, discussing academic books and research papers you have read, observations of provision and practice you have seen, ideas you are developing, or a draft essay you have written. Peer group support through telephone conversations, text messaging, email dialogue and social meetings are ways students support each other. This FD graduate reflects upon the support her study group gave her:

Reflective practitioner's voice

I reflected with others, there was a small group of us who stuck together, we carried on to the BA and helped each other.

Keeping a reflective journal

A reflective journal is valuable in supporting your reflective practice. This personal 'space' (Callan and Read, 2011: 84) is a place where you can record information, explore your feelings, issues, dilemmas, emotional and intellectual responses to challenges you face within your studies and work setting. By keeping a reflective journal you are able to think more deeply about issues (Bolton, 2005); the writing becomes an internal dialogue (Tsang, 2007) where individual reflective thinking takes place before sharing thoughts, ideas and emotions with others (Leeson, 2010). The journal can be in any form, a diary, a notebook, ring binder file or in an electronic format. It is important to write in it regularly to keep an ongoing 'discussion' with yourself (Callan and Read, 2011: 70).

The journal is a useful place to keep information you find from the Internet, magazines, newspapers and books, and can be annotated with your reflective thoughts. It is a reflective space and place to consider the session or lecture you have attended and to reflect upon your work placement or your daily work with children. Through reflective review, your learning informs your professional practice and academic development. The following questions for reflection will help in writing reflective reviews in your journal. In writing reviews it is important to record factual information (author, date, title of book/journal article, place of publication and page number) so you have the source of the evidence to reference in any essay you write (Rawlings, 2008). It is important to get into this habit for writing academically.

〜 Questions for reflection: *Reflective reviews*

The following questions will help you write reflective reviews about academic literature, research and information you have read and lecture sessions attended. They will help you identify areas of new learning, and link academic literature, theory and research to professional practice.

Reflective reading review

When writing a reflective review of academic literature or research, the following questions will help to structure your reflective thinking and learning.

> *First, record the title of the book, chapter number or research paper reference, so you can reference it correctly in any writing you do.*

- What have I learnt from my reading?

Summarize the key issues and identify key learning points.

- How has the reading informed my professional practice and/ or my role as a practitioner?

What do I need to do now?

- Is there any further reading to understand the topic more, or a question to ask my tutor, to build upon my learning from this reading?

Reflective information review

Information collected from a range of sources, such as television, newspapers, professional magazines, Internet, conferences, in-service courses or a comment from a parent or colleague, provides opportunity

(Continued)

(Continued)

to reflect upon current policy and practice, and to consider new learning and the impact upon your professional practice. When writing a reflective review of some information you have encountered, the following will help to structure your reflective thinking and learning:

- First, record the source of information, its topic and give it a title, so you can reference it correctly later.
- What have I learnt about the topic?

Summarize the key issues and identify key learning points.

- How has the information provided me with new ways of thinking?
- How will the information impact upon my professional practice and/or my role as a practitioner?

What do I need to do now?

- Is there any further reading or discussion I could do to build upon my learning from this information?

Reflective session review

These questions enable you to identify areas of new learning for professional practice from the sessions you attend:

- First, record the title and topic of the session, lecture, workshop, seminar or tutorial you attend, so you can reference it correctly later.
- What have I learnt about the topic?

Summarize the key issues and identify key learning points.

- How has the content of the session, lecture, workshop, seminar or tutorial attended, informed or impacted upon my professional practice and/or my role as a practitioner?

What do I need to do now?

- Is there one aspect of my reflective learning that I can use in my academic study or in my everyday work with children and families?
- Is there any further reading to understand the topic more, or a question to ask my tutor, to build upon my learning from the session, lecture, workshop, seminar or tutorial?

The process of gathering knowledge and reflecting upon it is a starting point for writing an essay. Writing in an academic style using critical analysis to develop argument and debate is now discussed.

Critical analysis

The academic writing style used in undergraduate and postgraduate essays should not describe information, provision and practice but critically analyse themes, issues and theories in light of academic literature, research, government policy and legislation, provision and practice. Academic writing combines knowledge and experience, the application of theory to professional practice in a critical cohesive discourse, demonstrating academic rigour (Rawlings, 2008). The transition from reflective writing, which can be predominantly about provision and practice and found in some FD assessments, to more theoretical writing found in the final stage of BA degrees, can be problematic for some students.

 This issue is discussed further in Chapter 5.

In writing essays from a critically reflective standpoint, the questions What? Why? Who? How? around provision and practice, theories, research evidence and improvement form a questioning framework for critical analysis, as shown in Figure 6.1. The questions when used deconstruct knowledge about a topic gained, provision and practice experienced.

What?	Why?	Who?	How?
What is current provision and practice?	Why is it in provision and practice?	Who has written about it?	How can this analysis inform, improve provision and practice?
What are the theories supporting provision and practice?	Why does it benefit children and families, practitioners?	Who has carried out research?	How can this analysis develop new theories?
What research evidence is there to support theory, provision and practice?	Why doesn't it benefit children and families, practitioners?	Who are the experts in the field?	How can this analysis develop new ways of working?

Figure 6.1   A Framework for Critical Analysis

The following critical analysis activity builds upon the questioning framework for critical analysis in Figure 6.1, supporting students in the process of critical analysis, from descriptive reflection to theoretical reflection, linking theory to practice.

∿ Questions for reflection: *Critical analysis activity*

A plastic bottle of water is required for this activity. The bottle of water is the focus for reflective questions which lead the participant through the process of critical analysis. The activity can be carried out individually or preferably with another, as through discussion further understanding of the process of critical analysis will emerge. If the activity is used as a class activity, a tutor facilitating feedback and whole group discussion at the end of the activity will enable further understanding of the process of critical reflection and analysis.

Put the bottle of water (known as the object) in front of you, this object forms the focus of your critical analysis, the questions will guide your analysis through discussion, make brief notes if you wish, engaging in the process of critical analysis is more important than making copious notes.

DESCRIBE IT

- What is it like?
- What colour is it?
- What shape is it?
- What height is it?
- What texture has it?

EVALUATE IT

- What is it made of?
- How was it made?
- Where was it made?
- Who has made it?
- What purpose does it have?

ANALYSE IT

Reflect upon:
- Its value.
- The importance of it as an object.
- Its purpose and usefulness.
- Why is it useful and important?
- What are its advantages or disadvantages?
- How has the object affected your life or that of others?
- Can it be improved?
- Can it be developed?

REFERENCES LINKING THEORY TO PRACTICE

- Has anybody written/said anything to support your thinking and understanding of the object?
- What has been written about the object or related subjects in academic literature, research journals?

- Are there any similar objects with similar or different uses?
- Where and how could you extend your knowledge about the object?

RECOMMENDATIONS

- Can you make any recommendations for modification, improvement and development?

The process of critical reflection and analysis uses various reflective lenses from academic literature, research, provision and practice, and personal and professional experience of the topic, this is deconstructed and reconstructed with new insights, ways of thinking and working with children, families and professionals.

Enjoying your studies

Studying in higher education is a unique experience which will open up new areas of knowledge, practice and research, furthering understandings in the field of early years and early childhood. It may be challenging at times and certainly hard work. However, it is important to engage in all opportunities and primarily enjoy your time for studying and learning. The chapter now discusses aspects of provision in higher education which support your academic and work-based reflective learning.

A reflective learning environment

Each student develops their own agency for study through the higher education learning environment they inhabit that fosters reflective learning. Figure 6.2 illustrates important components of the learning environment that develop the reflective self: reflective conversations; time and space for reflective thinking; writing as a process of reflection; being part of a community of learners and practice in higher education and within the workplace, and engaging in an academic and work-based learning partnership. All elements interact with each other, forming a holistic and encompassing reflective culture in which students can learn academically and vocationally.

The different elements shown in Figure 6.2 are discussed below, exploring how each enables work-based reflective learning and becoming

Figure 6.2　The Reflective Learning Environment

a reflective student. Although these elements were significant in the FD case study, they are relevant for all successful higher educational learning environments.

The reflective self

Central to becoming a reflective student is the reflective self. Effective educators are those who understand the importance of self-knowledge, undertaking self-study of themselves, their knowledge, feelings and the frameworks within which they understand children (Drummond, 2000). This learner-centred principle informed the design of two core modules in the FD case study, enabling the development of knowledge and understanding of reflection for professional learning. One module focused upon the self as a developing practitioner, providing a platform for developing self-knowledge and awareness both personally and professionally. Students demonstrated an understanding of their professional learning and development, identifying their work-based areas of expertise and areas for development.

You may be a student new to the early years or you may be an experienced practitioner working in the early years. The following questions will help you understand your personal and professional self, and identify your areas of personal and professional strength and areas for development.

 Questions for reflection: *The reflective self*

What roles do you have in your life?

There are many personal and professional roles in a person's life, as a mother, father, aunt, uncle, nephew, niece, carer, practitioner, teacher, leader, manager. Consider the family, work and social roles you have. Do they relate or connect to each other? If so how?

What experiences have you had in your life?

Everybody has many personal and professional experiences during a lifetime as a learner, carer and educator.

- List some of your key experiences as a learner, carer and educator.
- Consider how these experiences have influenced you.

    – How am I as a learner?
    – How am I as a carer?
    – How am I as an educator?

What are the contribution of your roles and experiences?

Consider how these roles and experiences influence your values and beliefs and your work with children, families and professionals.
    The next two questions help you consider your work as a practitioner or a student practitioner and identify areas for development.

What do I do well?

Consider the strengths of your work in the early years.

- What are you good at?
- What knowledge, skills and understanding do you have?
- What areas of experience and expertise do you have?

What do I need to develop?

Consider areas of your work for development.

- Where am I now?
- Where do I want to go?
- What knowledge, skills and understanding do I need to develop?
- What resources will help me?
- What long- and short-term goals do I need to get there?

Action planning for the reflective self

Action planning identifies professional needs, integrates reflection in a structured context in which self-analysis, diagnosis, planning and review can take place (Beaney, 2004). In developing an action plan the following aspects provide a structure for reflective review, identifying ways for professional improvement through the development of professional knowledge, skills and understanding. The following questions will help you in developing your own action plan for professional learning and development (Hallet, 2008b). Present your action plan in a narrative or a chart.

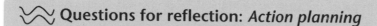 **Questions for reflection:** *Action planning*

- *Professional need target.* What professional knowledge, skills and understanding do I need to develop? How can this be developed into a specific achievable target?
- *Benefits.* Who will benefit from this development?
- *Resources.* What financial, environmental and human resources do I require to help me achieve this professional need target?
- *Timescale.* What amount of time is required to achieve the professional need target? The timescale should be broken down into small achievable steps; short-, medium- and long-term targets to completion date.
- *Evaluation.* How will I know that I have achieved my professional need target? What outcomes can be evaluated? How will these outcomes be evaluated?

Action planning is a process for practitioner agency. The agency of the reflective self in leading and implementing change is now discussed.

The reflective self as an agent for change

Another module in the FD case study focused upon the self as an agent for organizational change; students evaluated a work-based issue and reflectively considered how they led change in practice.

→ The leadership of change is discussed further in Chapter 8.

The following case study shows how a practitioner led change in her setting.

Case study: *Nursery and finger rhymes*

Imera is an early years practitioner working in a private day-care nursery. She has noticed that more children seem to have language delay than before and is concerned about how children's spoken language could be facilitated in her setting. She read the works of Marian Whitehead about children's spoken language as the foundation for learning and Linda Pound writing about the value of music in children's lives for developing listening skills, creativity and mathematics. These authors influenced her thinking. How could she raise the importance of children's listening skills and spoken language development through playful learning?

   She asked the nursery manager to add the issue to the next staff meeting agenda for discussion. Imera led the staff discussion by presenting a short paper with the rationale for developing children's listening skills and spoken language. During the discussion, the use of nursery and finger rhymes was highlighted as a way for children's spoken language and listening skills to develop. At the end of the discussion, Imera asked if the staff had any ideas to use in the nursery. The staff contributed several ideas, including holding a Nursery Rhyme Day for children and staff to dress up as their favourite nursery rhyme characters, and read and sing nursery and finger rhymes, and to invite parents to a workshop to make finger puppets, for use with their children at home. The staff were happy for Imera to organize the events to help the development of children's listening skills and spoken language.

The case study demonstrates the importance of sharing a work-based issue with others, being knowledgeable and inviting staff to be involved in providing solutions. The following questions will help you consider a work-based issue within your work setting, which you want to modify or change.

 Questions for reflection: *Reflecting on a work-based issue*

- What is the issue?
- What are the advantages and disadvantages of the work-based issue?
- What impact will the proposed change have for the staff, children, parents, and practitioners in the school, setting, children's centre or integrated service where you work?
- What impact will the proposed change have for your work as an early years practitioner?
- Why is it important to staff, children, parents, yourself, the school, setting, children's centre or integrated service in which you work?

The case study and reflective questions highlighted the importance of working as a reflective practitioner with others in a community of practice to change and improve practice. The value of students belonging to communities of learning and practice in higher education and work-based settings for academic and work-based reflective learning is now explored.

A community of learners and practice

In studying a higher education programme, each student joins a community of learners and practice at their study centre, which might be a university, further education college or a work-based outreach centre. The concept of a community of practice developed from work by Lave and Wenger (1991) concerns the social learning processes that take place when people with a common interest share ideas and practices, discuss issues, problem-solve, and develop shared understandings and new practices through reflective dialogue. A community of practice develops through participation and evolves over time, demonstrating that learning is not static but an emerging process of reflection for development, improvement and change in professional practice. Reflection has a capacity for transformation. Reflective practice loosens predictable outcomes, exposing the practitioner to new perspectives, possibilities and understandings (Moss, 2008a). The reflective culture and ethos established in the learning environment within a college or university is central to allowing reflection as an agent for personal and professional transformation.

To develop a learning community of reflective practitioners (Leeson, 2007) in which the learning becomes focused towards the practitioner as an individual, the teacher establishes a climate of trust and respect, facilitating practitioners to pursue and make meaning, develop their own theory, question practice and critique ideas from academic literature and research, thereby contributing to personal and professional learning through a reflective learning environment. Time and space within the learning environment for reflection are required. In the FD case study there was a supportive, reflective climate and pace in the sessions, allowing time and space for students to reflect upon practice, as this FD graduate's comment shows:

Reflective practitioner's voice

We brought things from our practice to discuss, sharing ideas and then tried to put new things into our practice. The delivery of the sessions allowed for reflection.

The learning community created was a uniquely gendered female one, all the students and tutors were women. This may have contributed to the establishment of a safe and non-threatening learning environment for the women practitioners who value relationships and work collegially (Rodd, 2006). This FD graduate reflects upon the learning community she experienced through her studies:

Reflective practitioner's voice

I developed confidence. I realized if I found something difficult I could talk to tutors, other students and work things out.

Meaningful, reflective conversations and dialogue with others sustain, nourish and raise individual and collective consciousness. They importantly involve a discussion of values and beliefs which is at the 'heart of the improvement process' (Leeson, 2007: 179).

The value of reflective conversations is a theme within the Model of Work-based Reflective Learning, ➔ discussed in Chapter 3.

Reflective practice requires a culture and belief that everyone has value to contribute to the community of learners to which they belong. Leeson (2010) regards a context that facilitates reflection and risk-taking should be in a college or university, for the creation of lifelong reflective practitioners, it should also be within the work setting. Work-based mentors who are located within the workplace contributed positively to students' learning on EYSEFDs (Knight et al., 2006; Robins, 2006) linking academic and work-based learning within an employer context. The importance of work-based mentors and their role in facilitating work-based reflective learning and practice within the work setting is now explored through the concept of a learning partnership.

Learning partnership

The work setting as a work-based community of practice forms an extension of the community of learning and practice found within the college or university study centre; a place where students can learn from practice and reflect with experienced practitioners through real contexts. In work-based contexts where time and reflective spaces are provided for practitioners to think, feel and talk about their work, there is great potential for reflective practice (Ruch, 2003). Academic and work-based learning communities of practice come together in a three-way learning partnership of the work-based mentor, student and study-centre tutor. This equal partnership supports practitioner work-based reflective learning within the work setting through mentoring pedagogy and the acquisition and achievement of professional and practical skills (Robins, 2006). The role of the work-based mentor as a 'critical friend' is as a critical but supportive colleague providing regular and ongoing feedback on practice (Knight et al., 2006). A critical friend will actively listen, question and challenge your knowledge and assumptions in a supportive and constructive way (Rawlings, 2008) 'encouraging the reflector to look beyond the superficial and think about their feelings and deeper learning' (Leeson, 2010: 188).

The engagement in the reflective process with others, a study partner, study group, work-based mentor or tutor, enables greater quality and deeper understanding of professional issues and practice (Leeson, 2010). Reflective collaborative dialogue is at the heart of the three-way learning partnership of the work-based mentor, student and tutor. There is equity within the learning partnership, each contributing equally in the partnership.

 Aspects of partnership working are discussed in Chapter One.

Regular communication and interaction between all three provides an enabling triangle for the student. The student's academic, professional progression forms the focus of a learning visit to the work setting by the study centre tutor. During this visit, reflective time and space are given for the student's progress to be reviewed, discussed and documented, and areas for development planned. Observations of practice from the work-based mentor, an extract from the student's reflective diary, a self-review can be used as focus for the student's progress review and reflective dialogue during the learning visit. The seven 'S's framework provides a structure for self-review. The framework provides ways for practitioners to reflect upon their role and how they support and facilitate children's learning (Hallet, 2008a: 78).

 Questions for reflection: *Self-review: the seven 'S's framework*

Reflect upon how you support and enable children's learning, you may like to select one area of learning, for example, talking, reading, writing, numeracy, science, creativity, or you may like to reflect upon how you support children's holistic learning and development. For each of the seven aspects of your role, give an example from your practice:

- Supplying – providing opportunities.
- Supporting – valuing, intervening, extending.
- Scaffolding – helping confidence and independence.
- Sharing – talking about, asking questions, engaging in sustained shared thinking.
- Showing – demonstrating, being a role model.
- Saying – praising, encouraging.
- Seeing – observing and planning for future learning.

A successful learning partnership not only benefits each student's learning and development but brings a reflective lens about the learning culture within the work setting for the work-based mentor. The learning visit can provide professional updating for the study-centre tutor within a current early years context. A learning partnership provides three perspectives to learning through reflective review, dialogue and documentation, enabling the development of a reflective student.

Summary

This chapter has explored ways to becoming a reflective student, providing practical advice for students starting to study at the beginning of their higher educational journey and as they travel to achieve their degree. Some significant aspects of a reflective learning environment in higher education have been considered; belonging to academic and work-based communities of learners and practice; a learning partnership of mentoring pedagogy and reflective dialogue for reflective review of academic and vocational progress.

The next chapter explores the development of practitioners' professional identity through work-based reflective learning.

Further reading

There is a useful guide to study skills in Chapter 3 of:
Rawlings, A. (2008) *Studying Early Years*. Maidenhead: Open University Press.

This book provides comprehensive information about mentoring within the early years context:
Robins, A. (ed.) (2006) *Mentoring in the Early Years*. London: Paul Chapman Publishing.

7

Reflecting upon Professionalism in the Early Years

Chapter overview

The introduction of workforce reform (DfES, 2005) and, in particular, the graduate professional award, Early Years Professional Status (EYPS) and the role of the Early Years Professional (EYP) as a professional leader of practice, introduced the notion of professionalism within the early years and the professionalization of the workforce. This chapter explores the evolving professionalization and emerging professional identity within the early years sector through higher education and professional training.

This chapter will:
- Examine the development of professionalism within the early years context.
- Discuss professional attributes and dispositions.
- Consider the contribution of reflective learning upon the development of professional identity.
- Examine emotional professionalism.
- Discuss emerging professionalism within integrated practice.

Professionalizing the early years workforce

Traditionally the workforce in the UK has been an under-qualified and underpaid group of working-class women, and training has been minimal (Vincent and Braun, 2010). The emphasis of professionalizing the early years workforce involves more and better training, a clearer framework for qualifications and an integrated early years service with a core of graduate practitioners and, over time, Level 3 becoming the minimum qualification for the early years workforce (Vincent and Braun, 2010: 204).

The development of Government policy and strategy for reform of the early years workforce has been discussed earlier in Chapter 1.

This chapter builds upon the earlier discussion, focusing upon the development of a graduate-led workforce through higher education and professional training and reflecting upon the implicit professionalization of the workforce.

In 2005, the Labour government set out 'to create and support a world-class workforce which is increasingly competent and confident to make a difference to the lives of those they support' (DfES, 2005: 1) to develop a higher qualified workforce and quality of provision particularly in the private voluntary and independent (PVI) sector. Early Years Professional Status is central to this strategy, a new professional status for graduate professional leaders of practice, who are to improve, shape and change practice, and lead and support others in their practice, particularly the Early Years Foundation Stage curriculum (EYFS) (CWDC, 2007). Early Years Professional Status is a nationally recognized graduate professional award, delivered through several training pathways. For practitioners to gain the graduate leader award, they are assessed by national standards for professional competence in sets of knowledge and understanding. These are: effective practice; relationships with children; communicating and working in partnership with families and carers; teamwork and collaboration, and professional development (CWDC, 2008). At the time of writing these standards are under review. The Nutbrown Review of Early Education and Childcare Qualifications highlights there should be clear and relevant pathways for practice-leaders through well-defined higher education and training routes (DfE, 2011c).

Internationally, results from the Organisation for Economic Co-operation and Development (OCED, 2006) highlighted the need for all countries to address professional education, status, pay and working conditions of early childhood staff to support quality, child outcomes, recruitment and retention of staff. Early Years Professional Status as a nationally recognized graduate leader award goes some way in addressing these issues, particularly in raising the status of those working in the early years, although increased recognition through an increased level of pay has yet to be addressed (Cooke and Lawton, 2008; Lloyd and Hallet, 2010). The purpose of the Nutbrown Review of Early Education and Childcare Qualifications (DfE, 2011c) is to develop further a high qualified early years workforce of skilled, knowledgeable professional practitioners. A key issue in the review is developing a suite of coherent qualifications which supports professionalism and motivation in the workforce so that learning takes place through high-quality practice experience, theory-based learning and critical reflection (DFE, 2011c).

The EPPE Project (Sylva et al., 2010) demonstrated the link between high-quality provision and highly qualified workforce, particularly in pre-schools led by qualified teachers and when teachers supervised others. The introduction of graduate professional status (EYPS) within the PVI sector aimed to give parity with Qualified Teacher Status (QTS), although in reality this has not been realized. Early Years Professional Status is not a qualification like QTS, therefore the award has been placed opposite to existing qualifications, such as those of an early years teacher or social worker (Lloyd and Hallet, 2010).

The notions of quality and professionalism tend to merge within policy discussions (Urban, 2008), certainly in relation to EYPS, professionalism is often associated with quality. The introduction of Early Years Professionals to raise the quality of provision in the PVI sector began to professionalise the early years workforce, previously not addressed. Peeters (2008) identifies dimensions of professionalism within childcare. Being professional means belonging to an expert group whose members have a unique body of knowledge, and there is restrictive entry and protected identity. The development of professionalism in childcare requires a nationally recognized qualification and the value of practitioners' work recognized and appreciated by government through better pay and conditions.

The government agenda for raising quality of provision in the PVI sector through the EYP role has set the context for practitioners to become 'professional' (Miller and Cable, 2011), raising the concern that practitioners without EYPS are not viewed as professional. Fenech and Sumison (2007) warn of 'othering' of less qualified practitioners. Osgood (2009: 739) identifies the construct of quality provision in England, as 'a regulatory framework of accountability, measurability and best practice via professional standards.' The National EYPS Standards provide an external prescription for professionalism within the early years workforce, under the government's regulatory gaze for standardization and accountability, there is developing a workforce of competent childcare technicians whose competencies, procedures and goals are being tightly prescribed through dominant constructions of professionalism externally given, rather than reflective competent and confident practitioners, reinforcing the culture of regulation and performance (Moss, 2008b; Osgood, 2006). This is in contrast to the image of the pedagogue in Europe, a democratic reflective professional with active agency (Moss, 2008b).

The voice of the early years workforce has been absent during the reform and development of a world-class workforce (McGillvray, 2008).

What would this world-class workforce look like? What are the characteristics of this workforce? These questions were given to practitioners studying a postgraduate early years degree, who all worked as teachers, early years practitioners, nursery nurses, teaching assistants and children centre leaders (in 2011). They were asked to present their views to the rest of the group. The following case study is one of those presentations.

Case study: *A world-class workforce – what should it look like?*

The four students presenting, Meera, Anthony, Caroline and Fin all work with children and families as a children's centre leader, reception teacher, nursery nurse and a teaching assistant.

We feel that all staff working with young children should be highly qualified and competent, knowledgeable of child development and the Early Years Foundation Stage curriculum. They should provide in settings, schools and children's centres a sound pedagogy of first-hand direct and play-based experiences, for children to have space and time to play and learn in well resourced areas, both inside and outside; to involve the family in children's learning and development.

The workforce should be well paid based upon their qualifications, to attract and keep staff with on-going career and professional development. There should be good and effective leadership from experienced and forward-thinking professionals, experienced staff to share their knowledge and skills with others. The workforce should be inclusive and diverse, in terms of gender, culture, age, ability and disability, a unified workforce working within a common agenda and goals for a holistic and integrated service, in a good environment that will support staff, children and families.

The following activity will help you reflect upon the views given in the case study.

Questions for reflection: *Developing a professional workforce*

From the practitioners' views in the case study:

- Are there any aspects of professionalism shown?
- Is a professional identity emerging?

There is a common understanding evolving, that to be a professional requires a high level of training and education (McGillvray, 2008). However, the development of professionalism is emerging from within the workforce through new understandings of professionalism (Miller and Cable, 2011). Early Years Professional Status training and EYP Network Groups have provided a forum for developing professional identity, collective voice and agency for these early years graduate leaders of practice (Hallet, forthcoming).

Defining professionalism within the early years

Over the past five years, the nature of professionalism in the early years is emerging through dialogue about professionalism by writers such as Osgood, McGillvray, Miller, Moss, Urban, Oberheumer and others. Dalli and Urban (2008: 131) view 'professionalism as a discourse as much as a phenomenon, something that is constantly under reconstruction'. Similarly, Friedson (1994) identifies professionalism as a changing phenomenon within a national context. Historically, professionalism has been part of the disciplines of sociology, medicine, education and law, but relatively new to the field of early years and early childhood. There is a lack of agreement as to the meaning of professionalism because it is conceptually complex; professionalism is not one concept but a cluster of related concepts (Aldridge and Evetts, 2003) such as being a professional, behaving professionally, working with professional autonomy, and having a professional identity.

Within the field of early childhood education and care (ECEC) there are diverse perspectives about professionalism. From a New Zealand perspective, Duhn (2011) considers that one type of professionalism does not fit all, arguing for professional knowledge-in-the-making and the learning self as a basis for professionalism which requires engagement with people, things, ideas, policies and politics as part of an ongoing discourse. From a German perspective, Oberhuemer (2005) recommends a model of democratic professionalism with four levels of professional activity: interacting with children; care management and leadership; partnership with parents; and knowledge base. This is a concept based upon participatory relationships and alliances for collaborative, co-operative action between colleagues and other stakeholders. Similarly, Moss (2008b: 125–126) argues that ECEC requires practitioners with activism to engage in and contest policy and practice, 'democratic and reflective practitioners' who are critical thinkers and researchers, constructors of meaning, identity and values, and practitioners who value participation, diversity and dialogue with others. Moss offers a common core of understanding and values for democratic professionalism:

- *Dialogue* – engaging in reflective conversations with other professionals develops thinking and practice.
- *Critical thinking* – engaging in questioning, encoding and challenging given facts and one's experience.
- *Researching* – investigating to make sense and construct meaning.
- *Listening and openness to otherness* – being open to differences and actively listening to other viewpoints.
- *Uncertainty and provisionality* – recognizing your identity is changing and evolving.
- *Subjectivity* – recognizing and taking responsibility for personal opinions.
- *Border crossing, multiple perspectives and curiosity* – being able to question and analyse culture with a critical eye.

The importance of practitioners being able to engage in reflection is central to the development of reflective and democratic professionals. Their education and continuous professional development should include the opportunity for them to deepen their understanding of the values and how to express them within their professional practice, 'assuming the responsibility to choose, experiment, discuss, reflect and change' (Moss, 2008b: 126). Reflection is included in the EYPS National Standards and graduate leader training. Candidates are required to reflect upon and evaluate the impact of their practice, modifying approaches where necessary (CWDC, 2007). Reflection and critical analysis particularly through journalling were found to be effective tools which helped practitioners to 'think through what to do next, or work out how things might be done better' in the evaluation of the National Professional Qualification for Integrated Centre Leaders (NPQICL) programme (National College for School Leadership, 2008: 7).

A 'reflective model of training' concerning the process of examining and exploring an issue of concern or a critical incident, triggered from experience, resulting in a changed perspective, identifies experience as the basis for reflection (Boyd and False, 1983: 222). This pedagogy for training moves the training provider from being an expert deliverer of knowledge, to a facilitator of reflection on practice (Tarrant, 2000) based upon Schon's (1983) notion of the reflective practitioner. In this model, reflective practice becomes a 'meeting place' between theory and practice (McMillan, 2009), a space in which students can make connections between practice and theory.

A group of 20 candidates undertaking EYPS training at a training provider in the Midlands region (in 2009) were asked to define their understanding of reflective practice by writing words on Post-it notes, demonstrating the meaning of reflection within their professional practice. The emerging themes analysis formed their collective view (Yin, 2003). Their reflections in the following case study demonstrate the powerful impact of reflection and reflective learning upon agency for improving professional practice as early years practitioners.

 Case study: *Reflective agency*

The words the EYPS candidates wrote down about reflection within the context of their professional practice are organized into a list, demonstrating their agency within their professional practice, ranging from superficial level of engagement at the top, to deeper-level engagement at the bottom of the list, highlighting the impact of reflective activism in changing practice. The role of the EYP as a change agent (CWDC, 2008) emphasizes the importance of being a reflective practitioner with agency.

Reflection means

- Looking at
- Discovering
- Evaluating
- Examining
- Analysing
- Looking deeper
- Critically investigating
- Developing
- Moving
- Bringing change
- Improving provision
- Improving quality.

The questions below will help you reflect upon your own activism within the work setting.

 Questions for reflection: *Reflective agency*

Think about your professional practice; consider the words in the list above. Is there an aspect of your practice you have actively examined, evaluated or investigated? How has this reflective engagement in practice improved, developed, enhanced or changed practice and improved quality of provision?

Professionalism in the early years is a changing, multi-layered and multifaceted phenomenon (Miller and Cable, 2011: 8). The chapter now considers the development of professional identity within the early years sector.

Developing professional identity

During initial training courses for childcare delivered in further education colleges, attention is given to the notion of professionalism by instructing students how to behave in a professionally accepted way in settings and schools while on work placement. This would include the type of dress to wear including a discreet display of jewellery, politeness in addressing staff, staffroom protocols, consideration of personal habits, such as smoking and chewing gum, attendance and punctuality. This information, alongside attending work placement, is part of the process of acquiring, interpreting and inhabiting a 'vocational habitus' (Colley, 2006), how students on childcare courses come to understand what it is to be a 'good' childcare practitioner (Vincent and Braun, 2010: 203). A range of collective dispositions as well as individual dispositions forms the 'vocational habitus' of personal and professional idealized and realized dispositions for working in childcare (Vincent and Braun, 2010). This forms the starting point for further development of professional identity within the early years workforce.

Professionalization of the workforce evolves from how groups within it view themselves as professionals. Professional identities are constructed through social and political discourses, government discourse of the construct of the child and childhood; and roles and responsibilities; influence of curriculum and pedagogy (Tucker, 2004). Professional identity results from the interaction between professional experiences of practitioners and teachers and the social, cultural and institutional environment in which they function on a daily basis (Court et al., 2009). In early years practice, the personal and professional are intimately intertwined. Both aspects give each other significance, and are inexorably linked to teacher and practitioner professional identity (Court et al., 2009).

Professionalism is part of the 'professional self'. Kelchtermans (1993) suggests significant aspects of the professional self comprise five separate but interrelated elements: self-image, self-esteem, job motivation, task perception and future perspectives. The development of self-image and self-esteem is contextually situated within the workplace. How we see ourselves and how others view us, within the workplace, such as mentors, supervisors, managers, leaders, peers and colleagues, influences our self-image and self-esteem (Miller and Cable, 2011).

The development of the 'learning professional' (Guile and Lucas, 1999) underpins professionalism and professional identity; a positive approach to continuing professional development and learning in which a practitioner seeks out opportunities to extend their professional understandings and skills sets, rather than being concerned solely with those already possessed. Extended rather than restricted professionalism provides transformational professional learning; access to higher education has transformed the agency of the workforce. The FD graduates in the case study redefined their professional identity through their higher educational learning. They had increased specialized knowledge, personal and professional confidence to work with other professionals who viewed them differently, as these themed comments demonstrate:

Reflective practitioners' voices

Professional identity

> I feel professional inside. The foundation degree gave me confidence and a professional identity. It's made me a different person in a professional role.

Others' perceptions

> Once I got the foundation degree, people saw me differently. I was no longer a nursery nurse but a professional person.

Developed confidence

> At the beginning of my job as a children's centre coordinator, I was seriously blagging it. I thought people would find out, I'm a nursery nurse and I'd say to someone 'Oh I've just said such and such!' But now I can do it, I will talk to anyone and give presentations to large groups.

Increased specialized knowledge

> I worked in a multidisciplinary setting and they needed professionals to work with families. You had to be more professional to equate with others across the service. The foundation degree gives you specialized knowledge to work with other professionals.

Professionalizing the early years sector

> The foundation degree is about what we do and how to make our professionalism better. It increases professionalization and helps to improve things and professionalize the sector.

Being valued

> It's good to be recognized in a profession.

> *Career progression*
>
> The foundation degree helped me up the professional ladder.

Some of the FD graduates in the case study progressed onto EYPS training programmes. Their views about professionalization of the workforce and professional identity were further explored and thematically analysed (Yin, 2003) in four themes (Lloyd and Hallet, 2010): professionalization of the workforce; professional identity; professional attributes; and belonging to a professional group. The graduate leaders in their training recognized the contribution of higher education and professional awards in raising the status of the early years workforce and the quality of provision for better educational outcomes for children. Through access to educational opportunities for professional learning they now felt more valued. The developing personal and professional characteristics of confidence, empowerment, pride and passion for working with children, improved professional status through the title 'Early Years Professional', change of job role and respect received from others, had influenced their emerging professional identity. The graduate leader training enabled self-knowledge through study and reflecting upon experience, providing professional attributes associated with leadership: being motivational, a role model to inspire others, enabling others in a passionate and inspirational way, shared understanding, developing a climate of trust, understanding and listening to others, being strategic, able to delegate, able to make decisions and take risks within a framework for improvement. Professional identity was developed through belonging to a professional group, in which shared understanding and vision developed cohesively, forming a collective voice and agency.

Emotional professionalism

The aspect of emotionality within professional identity is discussed within the theoretical framework of attachment theory. Bowlby's (1988) work on young children's emotional attachment to adults establishes the need for children to be cared for in order to thrive. Manning-Morton (2006) argues that caring physical interactions such as rocking and physical games with young children stimulate positive physical and intellectual development. Emotional detachment can inhibit practitioners from meeting young children's needs, particularly children under 3 years of age (Manning-Morton, 2006). Children naturally stimulate emotion and care in adults (Moyles, 2001). Parents respond to their children in emotionally and caring ways; therefore there is an expectation that this will continue in early years settings (Moyles, 2001). Students in their initial childcare training are encouraged to develop caring attributes such as sensitivity, warmth and emotionality. Colley (2006: 20) describes such dispositions as the 'unwritten curriculum' and part of practitioner advocacy for children. The term 'educare' highlights the integration of care with education (MacLeod-Brudenell, 2008). Working with children has physical, intellectual and emotional aspects for practitioners; emotionality within the workplace requires practitioners to manage their feelings to evoke particular feelings in others. This 'emotional labour' is influenced by social conditioning, education and training (Colley, 2006). Dealing with emotive situations on a daily basis and working with unpredictability in a calm and sensitive way and maintaining a level of appropriate detachment requires high-level thinking achievable only through experience and training (Moyles, 2001). For practitioners to maintain an appropriate professional intimacy, making every child feel special, while keeping an appropriate professional distance, requires emotional work of the highest calibre (Moyles, 2001). Osgood (2011) views emotional labour as a sophisticated skill capable of providing practitioners with a sense of empowerment.

Emotional labour has impacted upon practitioner identity in respect of gender and socio-economic class. Research by Vincent and Braun (2010) found the majority of practitioners in the early years workforce were female and from socio-economically disadvantaged backgrounds. Working with children in education and care provided opportunities for low-status marginalized groups of women to reinvent themselves within a morally prestigious occupation. Students on childcare college courses value work with young children as it provides them with an opportunity to give something back (Vincent and Braun, 2010). Colley (2006) found that emotional labour can develop self-worth, respectability and provide practitioners with a feeling of higher stature. Emotional labour and an ethic of care are significant in terms of group and professional identity. Traditionally there has been a view that working with children is associated with women's role of working with children, and emotional labour is specifically 'women's way of knowing' (Taggart, 2011: 91). However, early years practitioners work confidently and appropriately with care and emotion in their daily work with children and families. Hargreaves and Hopper (2006) suggest that professionalism and improved status will be more achievable if teaching rather than care is repositioned as central to quality in early childhood education. Osgood (2006) believes that practitioners should confidently embrace an ethic of care and emotional labour, as part of their professional identity and emerging professionalism.

Professionalism within integrated practice

The implementation of government policy as Every Child Matters (DfES, 2004) and recently early intervention (Allen, 2011) has required co-operative and collaborative multi-professional working across professional and organizational boundaries at strategic and organizational levels. Through the development of integrated practice in which a range of professionals work together putting policy into practice, professionalism for professionals working in interdisciplinary teams in settings such as children's centres, family centres, schools, health centres and across a range of local authority children's services is emerging (Brock and Ranklin, 2011). Each group of educational, health and social care practitioners brings its own professional identity, values and working practices to a larger professional team. The development of professionalism within the interdisciplinary early years team has been considered by Brock (2011: 69–70). She identifies seven dimensions of professionalism: knowledge, education and training; skills, autonomy, values, ethics, reward – and each dimension has dimensional traits. The seven dimensions of professionalism are shown in Figure 7.1.

The seven dimensions of professionalism	The dimensional traits
Knowledge	Knowledge gained through study of varying theoretical frameworks including child development; how children think and learn; curriculum and pedagogy. Knowledge gained through experience of working with young children and their families. Knowledge gained through experience of children's social and cultural backgrounds and their individual needs. Knowledge of local and national policy and implications for practice.
Education and training	Qualifications gained through further and higher education and apprenticeship through working with children, applying knowledge to practical experience. Self-directed continuing professional development to further develop knowledge and expertise. Appropriate training with regard to young children's learning and development. Training to deliver flexible curriculum and high level of pedagogic knowledge.

(Continued)

Figure 7.1 (Continued)

Skills	Planning curriculum and teaching particularly through play-based pedagogy. Observing and assessing young children's learning and development. Monitoring and evaluating effectiveness to inform practice and provision; able to critique, reflect and articulate understanding and application. Multidisciplinary skills that encompass the demands of the role. Effective team work with different professionals, creating an inclusive ethos for children and families. Ability to make judgements regarding appropriate practice and dealing with problems. Effective communication of aims and expectations to stakeholders of families, colleagues, advisers, governors, and Ofsted.
Autonomy	Recognition of specific professional knowledge and expertise regarding young children's learning and development. Autonomy over professional responsibilities and allowed to use discretionary judgement. Able to provide what they see as appropriate curriculum and pedagogy for their particular groups of children; stronger voice and consultation in the shaping of relevant policy and practice that affect young children's education and care. Recognition of professionalism, promoting status and value in the field of ECEC. Vocational aspects of working with young children recognized and endorsed.
Values	Sharing of a similar ideology based on appropriate knowledge, education and experience. Strong belief in teaching and learning through a play-based curriculum. Beliefs in principles for appropriate provision that meets children's and families' needs. Commitment to professional values and vocation built on moral and social purposes. Public service and accountability to the community and client group of children and families. Creating an environment of trust and mutal respect inherent in professional role. Self-regulating code of ethics applied to everyday working practices.
Ethics	Ethical principles and engaging with values regarding young children's education and care. High level of commitment to professional role and the client group of parents, carers and children. Collaborative and collective behaviour with colleagues in the setting and with other professionals. Inclusiveness while valuing diversity in all working relationships, including children, families and communities. Self-regulating code of ethics applied to everyday working practice.
Reward	Personal satisfaction, interest and enjoyment in working with young children. Forming strong and supportive relationships with young children and families. Strong commitment for the professional role and to own professionalism. Being valued and gaining acclaim for the professional expertise from colleagues and policy-makers. Financial remuneration through appropriate salary.

Figure 7.1   The Seven Dimensions of Professionalism

These seven dimensions of professionalism can be used as a framework for reflection as suggested in the following activity.

 Questions for reflection: *Seven dimensions of professionalism*

Reflect upon the seven dimensions of professionalism and the dimension traits in Figure 7.1. For each dimension of professionalism reflect in relation to your own professionalism.

- What areas of professional experience and expertise do you have?
- What areas of professionalism do you identify for development?

 Summary

The chapter has explored and reflected upon the development of professionalism within the early years sector through an examination of workforce reform, the formation of a reflective graduate workforce, and emerging interdisciplinary professionalism. Influences upon the development of professional identity have been discussed, including emotional professionalism particular to the early years. There has been opportunity to reflect upon case studies as examples from practice, and to reflect upon emerging professional identity and developing professionalism.

The next chapter furthers the discussion about professionalism and professional identity through a focus upon reflective leadership.

Further reading

The following books provide an in-depth discussion of professionalism in the early years and children's services:

Brock, A. and Ranklin, C. (2011) *Professionalism in the Interdisciplinary Early Years Team*. London: Continuum.

Miller, L. and Cable, C. (2008a) *Professionalism in the Early Years*. Abingdon: Hodder Education.

Reflective Leadership

┌───┐
Chapter overview

This chapter examines defining leadership characteristics, style, practices and behaviours of early years leaders within the context of a developing graduate-led early years sector. The reflective thinking and learning skills required for leading within, across and beyond early years settings, schools, children's centres and children's services as a reflective leader are explored.

  This chapter will:
- Examine the development of a graduate-led early years sector.
- Discuss defining characteristics of leadership in the early years including the issues of gender.
- Discuss early years leaders' style, practices and behaviours.
- Examine transformational leadership.
- Explore leading and sustaining change for continuous improvement:
- Consider ways of developing your own leadership reflectively.

└───┘

Developing a graduate-led early years sector

The development of a graduate-led workforce has evolved over the past 20 years through government review of provision and research. The Rumbold Report (DES, 1990) and the Effective Provision of Pre-school Education (EPPE) (Sylva et al., 2010) significantly influenced the development of a graduate-led workforce. Starting with Quality: The Rumbold Report (DES, 1990) found inequalities in provision for 3- and 4-year-olds nationally, recommending the development of a workforce with higher qualifications to raise the standard of provision for children and families. The Rumbold Report (DES, 1990) introduced a multi-professional approach to service delivery through integrating care and education. The EPPE project (Sylva et al., 2010) found there was higher overall quality provision in settings that integrated care and education. The key characteristics of settings where children made better all-round progress were strong leadership, a trained teacher acting as a manager, supervising less-qualified practitioners and where a good proportion of staff were graduate qualified. These studies made a clear connection between highly qualified staff who were graduate leaders and high-quality provision for children and families.

During the time of these studies, the majority of young children were taught by qualified graduate teachers in nursery schools, classes or units attached to primary schools, as they still are today. In current early years provision young children have their education and care in a range of provision; in maintained state provision (schools) and non-maintained state provision (private, voluntary and independent) in schools, full and sessional day care, children's centres, playgroups, pre-schools and home-based child minders. A 4-year-old child can access the Early Years Foundation Stage curriculum by attending a school, children's centre or PVI setting. However, the practitioners they interact with have different qualifications and training. The majority of graduate leaders who are qualified teachers work in nursery and primary schools. There are a significant number of practitioners working in non-maintained (PVI) early years settings qualified to Level 3 with a growing number of graduate-level Early Years Professionals (EYP).

The Children's Workforce Strategy (DfES, 2005) attempted to address the imbalance of qualifications through the introduction of EYPs as graduate leaders of practice (CWDC, 2006) with the intention for EYPs to be teacher equivalent. In reality this hasn't been realized due to opposition from within the sector (Lloyd and Hallet, 2010). The EYP has a transformational leadership role to act as a 'change agent' to improve and lead practice across the EYFS curriculum, and to support and mentor other practitioners in effective practice (CWDC, 2008). Early Years Professionals, as leaders of practice, are to shape, and improve provision within the PVI sector, raising quality and equity of provision within, across and beyond early years settings.

→ EYP graduate leadership training and role are discussed in the previous chapter within the context of professionalizing the early years workforce.

Leadership in the early years

Leadership in the early years has been carried out within educational contexts by nursery school head teachers, teachers in nursery schools, classes and units, reception teachers and foundation stage co-ordinators, and continues to be so. There has been a general reluctance for early years leaders to recognize leadership as part of their professional role (Kagan and Bowman, 1997; Rodd, 2006) and identify themselves as leaders.

The introduction of higher educational professional awards through national leadership training programmes for SureStart children's centre leaders (NPQICL) and leaders of early years practice (EYPS) has raised the profile and status of leadership in the early years and broadened leadership roles and responsibilities. Leadership in the early years is emerging through the changing early years landscape with these professional awards and with the widening of children's services from school-focused educational outcomes to inclusion of social and health outcomes within integrated practice. Leadership in the early years is a complex phenomenon 'like a ball of knotted string' (Friedman, 2007: 142) that has to unravel for understanding. Bennis and Nanus (1997: 4) describe leadership as 'an abominable snowman, whose footprints are everywhere but nowhere to be seen'. This image represents leadership in the early years which has been happening, for example in nursery schools, without a comprehensive understanding of the leadership practices involved. The ball of string is beginning to unravel through research studies such as Effective Leadership and Management in the Early Years (Moyles, 2006), Effective Leadership in the Early Years Sector: The ELEYS Study (Siraj-Blatchford and Manni, 2007), Leadership of Learning in Early Years and Practice (The LLEAP project) (Hallet, forthcoming) and the Longitudinal Study of EYPS (Hadfield et al., 2011).

To implement government policy effectively into practice, Rodd (2006) highlights the need for effective childhood leadership. The EYP as a graduate leader of practice (Whalley, 2008) raises the importance of early years leaders and their contribution to children's learning and development. Nelson (2011: xi) highlights that young children 'deserve the best leaders to prepare them for the challenges they will face as they move forward into adulthood'.

The Longitudinal Study of EYPS indicates the positive impact of graduate-led leadership in effecting change and improving early years provision, particularly for those in their early career (Hadfield et al., 2011). The current Coalition government is committed to raising the qualifications and skills of the early years workforce and will further develop graduate early years leaders 'to help give every child the chance to thrive in their earliest years' (Teather, 2011: 11). The Nutbrown Review of Early Education and Childcare Qualifications (DfE, 2012) builds upon evidence in the Tickell Review of the Early Years Foundation Stage curriculum (EYFS) (2011) of a steady improvement in the skills of the early years workforce, supporting the understanding of the connection between a well-qualified, skilled, professional early years workforce and children's healthy development (Nutbrown, 2011b).

Gender and leadership

Women traditionally work in service jobs and historically associated female professions such as nursing and school teaching (Carli and Eagly, 2011). The majority of the early years workforce are female (Kay, 2005) but, although women are becoming better educated than men, there are more male than women leaders within schools, early years settings, children's centres and children's services. However, through higher education degrees and professional awards, a body of women leaders is emerging in front-line leadership roles (Lumsden, 2008) in early years settings, children's centres, children's services, integrated practice and schools. Educational opportunities and the development of employment opportunities in diverse services have enabled women to undertake leadership roles and responsibilities, as this FD graduate's vocational progression shows:

Reflective practitioner's voice

I now manage a team of eighteen, without the foundation degree I wouldn't have got the job as it was a requirement for it.

Carli and Eagly, (2011: 108) consider the gender gap in leadership not in terms of greater domestic and family responsibilities for women, but in terms of expectations of leadership behaviours for men and women. Research in the United States and other nations (Newport, 2001; Williams and Best, 1990) indicates that people expect men to be 'agentic', that is, assertive, dominant, competent and authoritative, and for women to be 'communal', that is, warm, supportive, kind and helpful. People also expect managers and leaders to be more agentic than communal. It is perceived that agentic leadership qualities are more conducive to men than to women, and the stereotype of effective leaders being assertive and male emerges. The challenge for women leaders is to balance the two traits, the demand for agency and the demand for communal leadership.

The construct of effective leadership is developing from a person who singularly makes decisions to drive the organization, to the construct that successful leadership is the ability to form good relationships with others, work in diverse teams, and influence and motivate others to make valuable and creative contributions to their organization (Carli and Eagly, 2011). A leader influences and empowers others to shape, improve and transform settings and services through supporting and enabling the leadership qualities of others. The chapter now considers this emerging construct of leadership within the early years context.

Early years leaders as transformational leaders

Recent reviews and reforms such as Every Child Matters (2004), the Children's Plan (2007) and the Allen, Field and Tickell reviews (2010 and 2011) are changing relationships between practitioners, education and society. The reforms and reviews have introduced new leadership roles within the early years sector, requiring new leadership approaches such as distributed, transformative and sustainable leadership, offering opportunities for leadership to be shared among teams, for example, leading the EYFS curriculum, a phase, safeguarding or family support team.

Transformational leaders both influence and are influenced by followers, they not only lead but also develop leaders. The effectiveness of their leadership is measured by the degree of social or cultural change that develops as a result of their leadership (Diaz-Saenz, 2011: 300). Bass (1985) identified four leadership behaviours in transformational leadership: idealized influence, inspirational motivation, intellectual stimulation and individualized consideration. Leaders with idealized influence become role models that others want to follow and even emulate. Leaders who create inspirational motivation, form a clear vision and pathway through which they inspire and enable a team to achieve the vision. Leaders who show intellectual stimulation encourage others to be innovative and creative, addressing and solving problems in new ways and examining existing assumptions. Leaders who show individual consideration are concerned with each follower as an individual, considering their individual needs abilities and aspirations, helping individuals to develop their strengths through coaching, guiding and mentoring (Diaz-Saenz, 2011).

These leadership behaviours are important in leading a multidisciplinary team and in leading change for setting, school, children's centre or service improvement. The key functions of a team leader are to create and communicate a vision to the group, develop a team culture, set goals, monitor and communicate the team's achievements to the team and relevant others, and facilitate and encourage the development of others, particularly in their leadership knowledge and behaviours. Effective team leadership and team-building usually results in high-quality interaction between the team members and the leader, increases trust and openness and develops interpersonal relationships and shared understanding. This team approach to working supports the professional development of staff, as experience and expertise are shared within the team. It can also support the 'challenge of change', providing a support structure for quality service delivery (Rodd, 2011: 275).

Collaborative leadership

The development of leadership within, across and beyond a setting, school or children's centre team requires each leader to have confidence, knowledge and expertise not only as a specialist in their area but in leadership pedagogy; to be confident in their own area of expertise and leadership and to value the contribution of others, being able to cross multi-professional barriers to develop understanding and professional trust. This model of leadership, required in an integrated practice team, is not of a leader who others follow, but of leadership focused on how well the leader articulates, shares the vision and distributes leadership to produce desired outcomes (Duffy and Marshall, 2007). Effective leadership is essential to ensuring a strong ethical underpinning of early years values to service provision. Rodd (2006) describes this style of leadership as collaborative, collegiate and democratic. Siraj-Blatchford and Manni (2007) note leadership in the early years seems to be as a result of groups of people working together to influence and inspire others, rather than the focus of one person acting as a single leader.

An empowering, collaborative style of leadership developed through a relational culture is associated with women rather than a more directive authoritarian style associated with men (Carli and Eagly, 2011). Being a leader within a multi-agency team offers an opportunity to develop and support leadership of others. Effective and empowering leadership acts as advocacy for young children. Leaders in multi-agency teams have the valuable task of acting as role models for future leaders, as well as ensuring the well-being of children (Duffy and Marshall, 2007).

Leadership for learning

The primary goal of an early years setting, school or children's centre should be to improve educational, social and health outcomes for children (Siraj-Blatchford and Manni, 2007). Early years leaders should be able to lead teaching and learning, and lead and support others in knowledge and understanding, effective practice, relationships with children, communicating and working in partnership with families and carers and in professional development (CWDC, 2008).

The Effective Leadership in the Early Years Sector: The ELEYS Study researched effective leadership for learning within the early years sector. The notion of 'leadership for learning' is articulated in the ELEYS Study (Siraj-Blatchford and Manni, 2007: 12). The study identified three *leadership qualities* in effective settings:

- contextual literacy
- a commitment to collaboration
- a commitment to the improvement of children's learning outcomes.

The ELEYS Study also identified a range of categories for *effective leadership practice*:

- Identifying and articulating a collective vision
- Ensuring shared understandings
- Effective communication
- Encouraging reflection
- Monitoring and assessing practice
- Commitment to ongoing, professional development
- Distributed leadership
- Building a learning community and a team culture
- Encouraging and facilitating parent and community partnerships
- Leading and managing: striking a balance.

The ELEYS Study was used as a framework for analysis in a research study investigating early years leaders' style and practices. The Leadership of Learning in Early Years and Practice (The LLEAP project) examined the leadership of practice role EYPs undertook in one local authority and found they had a specialist pedagogical role in the Leadership of Learning in a range of settings within the non-maintained sector (PVI) (Hallet, forthcoming). Their leadership style is a holistic and encompassing style; nurturing, caring and influencing, using a democratic, diffused and collaborative leadership style, inclusive of the whole community of children, parents and carers, and practitioners. Through further examination of their leadership of learning style, seven leadership of learning practices were identified;

- Leading whole setting pedagogy
- Leading pedagogy for children

- Leading knowledge within the setting
- Leading continuous professional learning
- Leading knowledge with parents and carers
- Leading change for setting improvement
- Leading reflection for learning.

The research gave an insight into early years leadership in settings other than schools within the non-maintained sector, revealing a pedagogical leadership role comparative to early years teachers (Lloyd and Hallet, 2010). The graduate leaders in the research identified the importance of the higher education training programme (EYPS) and continuing professional development opportunities to meet with other early years leaders in network meetings. During the research, early years leaders were invited to take part in reflective workshops which formed focus group discussions. At the 'Change Workshop' early years leaders were asked to bring an example of change they had implemented within their setting. During the workshop they used art and collage materials to visually represent the change process. Through focus group discussion these images were used for the early years leaders to deconstruct how they led and implemented change within their setting. An early years leader reflects upon the experience:

Reflective practitioner's voice

It has been fascinating to see all the variety of leadership and change taking place in settings with EYPs. I did wonder when I did the EYPS training course whether it would make a difference to settings and leadership – but today, the Change Workshop has shown me there are people out there with vision and commitment and sound philosophy. I have learnt so much from others today – it is wonderful to have that experience as often on courses I feel we don't gain anything extra. This surely means that we must take this forward, meeting, socializing and training other early years leaders.

Leading change for continuous improvement

A graduate early years leader's role is to be a change agent to improve and shape practice (CWDC, 2006) as a leader of practice (Whalley, 2011) first, by identifying a need for change to benefit children's learning and development within the setting; then establishing a clear vision based upon a sound pedagogy of specialized early years knowledge and experience of working with children, parents, practitioners and professionals. Effective leaders are reflective people with a sense of agency who become change-makers within their work contexts and more widely within their professional field (Costley and Armsby, 2007). Through reflective practice, practitioners have the potential to transform what they do and what children and families experience (Paige-Smith and Craft, 2011) and have agency for professional change in pedagogy, provision and professional practice. An effective leader ensures all colleagues are part of the change process, leading collaboratively through professional dialogue underpinned by early years knowledge and values (Colloby, 2009). The following case study demonstrates the effective use of reflection in leading change; identifying a need for change to improve provision for educational, social and health outcomes for children, implementing, monitoring and sustaining change.

 Case study: *Leading reflective change*

Claire is a teacher in a nursery school and is studying part-time on a postgraduate course. This writing is an extract from her essay about reflective practice, she reflects upon an example of her professional practice, introducing 'Learning Journeys' as an assessment tool. She reflects upon leading change in pedagogy and practice within her nursery.

> I began to reflect upon the effectiveness of our systems of observation and assessment which were routine and carried out daily. I began to feel there were many problems with the system we used; the majority of practitioners' time was taken up by writing observations rather than interacting with the children in the nursery. The observations recorded were out of context and not used in a meaningful way to help children's learning and development. There were issues about parental engagement and the organizational system was not providing a true indication of each child's learning experiences. Overall there was not a very effective or holistic approach for the recording or the nurturing of each child's learning and development.
>
> During my master's course, I learnt about the work of Margaret Carr in New Zealand and the assessment process of recording children's learning in 'learning stories'. These seemed purposeful observations forming a meaningful narrative focusing on learning dispositions and supporting children in their learning to learn. Through reflective thinking I wanted to:
>
> - increase the interactions between practitioners and children and ensure the interactions are meaningful for both the child and the adult
> - record further learning and development more effectively
> - involve parents and carers more in their child's learning and development, therefore creating an effective dialogue between the home learning environment and the nursery for the children.

For me to introduce change in the way practitioners observed and recorded, I realized that I should invite staff into reflective dialogue to include the perspectives of the practitioners I work with, the senior management team and parents and carers. I introduced my own reflections through a series of phase and team meetings, and at a workshop with parents and carers, I welcomed feedback and discussion. Through the dialogue we were able to collaboratively make meaning of our observation routine and the desire for change was agreed. Through dialogue we were able to engage in a reflective process of thinking and learning together, exploring our pedagogical approach to observation and assessment, reflecting upon our role as practitioners and interactions with children, parents and carers. We discussed the need for practitioners to be curious with children, to use language to encourage children's critical thinking through open-ended questioning and sustained shared thinking for practitioners and children to make meaning together to facilitate children's learning and development in a creative way. The focus of observation and assessment being on the process or the story of how children learnt, rather than the outcome or product of what they had learnt.

We then devised an accessible and contextualized format for recording children's learning stories, ensuring it was inclusive and accessible to their families. The format included a description of what happened in the form of photographs and narrative which inferred the learning and meaning-making that occurred. We were mindful of creating a flexible format for documenting interaction that would facilitate each practitioner's creative practice and prevent this change from becoming another checklist to complete, but a meaningful documentation of each child's learning and development.

This wasn't the end of the reflective process as effective change in setting provision is a continuous process of reflection, testing change through listening, dialogue and then reconstruction of new meanings and understandings. In implementing the change, problems arose to be solved. Time management was an issue, allowing time and space for reflection and interpretation of children's learning and development in the learning story was a major concern for practitioners, as was the levels of expectation placed on some practitioners to record and have the ability to reflect upon the learning that took place.

Through the dialogic process of 'reflection-on-action' as described by Donald Schon, I forged new understandings of my professional practice and effective setting provision. I learnt to be an effective leader of change: a dialogue needs to occur in which practitioners are listened to and are able to share perspectives and ideas. Practitioners need to take ownership over their practice in order to maintain positive and effective relationships between themselves, with children, parents and other professionals in order to contribute positively to setting provision.

The parents and carers in the setting have generally responded positively to the learning stories, in particular to the value placed on the home learning

(Continued)

(Continued)

environment and to being more involved in their children's learning and development. Parents are able to contribute to their child's learning story. This has led to increased engagement in family school trips and learning workshops in the nursery. The opening up of dialogue between the home and the nursery school has enabled relationships to become stronger quicker between nursery practitioners and families, and between children and practitioners.

There now exists in our nursery school a more effective provision and recording of the children's learning and development in purposeful ways that value and build upon the children's existing knowledge and experiences in a meaningful way for the children and their families and practitioners, helping them to plan for the children's next steps in their learning and development. Through the dialogic process of reflection and being listened to, relationships have strengthened between the nursery practitioners and communication is more effective.

As a reflective practitioner, I would argue that reflective practice contributes positively to setting provision, the reflecting on the 'why' and 'how' we are doing something is necessary to implement effective change and progress.

In the case study, Claire has shown the importance of reflection in the process of change. The following reflective activity will help you reflect upon a change process you have been involved with.

〰️ Questions for reflection: *Reflective change*

Reflect upon a change you have led within your setting, school or service or a change you have been involved in.

- What was the change?
- How were you involved in the change process, as a leader or team member?
- What did you do?
- How effective was the change?
- Has the change been sustained, is it still with your practice, setting, school or service provision?
- If yes, how is the change being monitored and maintained over time?

Developing your own reflective leadership

Reflection enables improvement in practice, solving problems and learning from experience (Jones and Pound, 2008). As the case study shows, Claire as an early years leader was reflective in her thinking and behaviour, and facilitated reflection within her staff team. The process of reflective practice is transformational and reflective leaders engage in reflective dialogue with others to change and modify practice. Effective leaders are reflective practitioners who lead by example, in modelling practice and behaviours and influencing others. They are reflective in their own practice and encourage reflection in their staff (Siraj-Blatchford and Manni, 2007). The leader establishes the reflective culture. An early years setting, school or children's centre with collaborative reflective processes at the centre is evolving and changing.

Early years leaders have responsibility for developing their own leadership style and practices through critical reflection and self-review within a framework of continuous professional learning, identifying their leadership strengths and areas for development. Their leadership identity is developed through the work context and the colleagues they interact with. Sinclair (2011: 509) describes how an 'authentic' leadership identity can be developed through biographical self-narrative, composing and telling a story about oneself. Leadership used to be task orientated but now it is an identity.

The experiences of leadership you encounter during your working life, positive and negative, can influence your own leadership style, behaviours and practices, and influence your leadership identity. The following questions will help you reflect upon influences on your leadership style, practices, behaviours and your identity as a leader.

〰〰 **Questions for reflection:** *Leadership identity*

Identify a leader who has positively influenced your professional and leadership development.

- What aspect of this leader's leadership qualities, style, practices and behaviours influenced you?
- What did you learn from the leader about being an effective leader?
- How has this experience influenced your leadership and identity as an early years leader?

Identify a leader who you regard as having poor leadership qualities, style, practices and behaviours.

- What aspect of this leader's leadership qualities, style, practices and behaviours affected you?

(Continued)

(Continued)

- What did you learn from the leader about being an ineffective leader?
- How has this experience influenced your leadership and identity as an early years leader?

Who am I? Write a sentence or short paragraph that describes your identity as an early years leader.

 Summary

The chapter has discussed defining characteristics of leadership in the early years through examining the development of a graduate-led sector. The uniqueness and influence of gender within a predominantly female workforce and their leadership roles in leading policy into practice have been considered. Research studies have illuminated early years leaders' style, practices and behaviours, particularly as transformational leaders in leading change for continuous improvement in provision and practice and in the leadership of learning. The second part of the chapter focused on the importance of early years leaders to be reflective of their own leadership style, practices and behaviour, and to establish a leadership identity and develop as reflective leaders within a framework of continuous professional learning.

Further reading

This book concerns a research study about leadership in the early years. A DVD in which graduate leaders reflect upon their leadership style and practices is included in the book, as a professional learning resource for existing and aspiring early years leaders:

Hallet, E. (forthcoming) *Leadership of Learning in Early Years and Practice* (The LLEAP project). London: The Institute of Education, University of London.

This book is a research report of the Effective Leadership in the Early Years Sector (ELEYS Study):

Siraj-Blatchford, I. and Manni, L (2007) *Effective Leadership in the Early Years Sector: The ELEYS Study.* London: The Institute of Education, University of London.

Reflective Learning Journeys

Chapter overview

Reflective learning and how students and practitioners engage in it has been threaded throughout the chapters of the book. In this chapter, examples of experienced women practitioners' reflective learning journeys through their higher educational experience of the foundation degree case study are shared. Key influences upon the graduates' academic, vocational and career progression are identified. Through autobiographical storying and reflection upon their learning journeys, the women's voices were heard as they travelled along the pathway to professionalism. The women's reflective voices about their individual and unique learning journeys aim to inspire students and early years practitioners to begin or continue their journey into learning.

This chapter will:
- Share women graduates' reflective learning journeys.
- Identify key transformational influences upon women's academic, vocational and career progression.

Women's journeys into reflective learning

Many women practitioners working in the early years sector have worked with young children for many years. Although experienced practitioners, many have had little access to higher education. Since 2006 the government has provided funding through the Transformation Fund and the Graduate Leader Fund to help raise qualifications of the early years workforce (DfE, 2011a). The funding allowed practitioners to study foundation and undergraduate degrees and the graduate leader award (EYP), widening access and engagement in higher education for many practitioners, particularly women, many of whom choose to study part-time. They begin their learning journey after time out of studying and this can seem daunting; studying at a university or in a further education college can seem huge and unfamiliar. The students walk down several pathways on their learning journey and on to graduation. These pathways are emotional, academic, personal and professional (Rawlings, 2008), and reflective. At the end of their learning journey, graduates have developed personally and professionally. Work-based learning graduates in Rawling's (2008) study had become independent learners, researchers, influencing practice, challenging and questioning issues and concerns, collecting evidence from informed good practice. Their developed confidence enabled them to progress their careers and further their qualifications.

Similarly in the FD case study, practitioners' reflective thinking about their professional views and experiences contributed to the formation of their professional identity, career progression and lifelong learning. By reflecting upon personal and professional histories, practitioners are able to make sense of influences and construct values, beliefs and pedagogy for working with children, families and multi-professionals. Clough and Corbett (2000: 156) describe this concept as 'lived relationships', 'lived experience' and personal and professional 'journeys'. Practitioners' distinctive and influential perspectives are determined by what they learn both personally and professionally over time. Personal and professional aspects of teachers' and practitioners' life histories are intimately intertwined, giving each other significance, and contributing to the development of professional identity (Court et al., 2009). Learning is developed through experience, and practitioners link analytical and reflective thinking to their own experience of practice (Paige-Smith and Craft, 2011). Reflective learning informs reflective practice. Reflective practice is a 'never-ending learning journey' involving personal and professional qualities and attributes as the individual becomes part of a community of early years practice (Appleby, 2010: 9). As practitioners increase their specialized knowledge and understanding of theory and practice, these become reference points for examining professional practice through reflective thinking and learning. Through this process practitioners become 'reflective professional practitioners' (Moss, 2008b).

The learning journey of women graduates in the FD case study was examined. The concluding finding in the research study found that they had developed into 'reflective professional practitioners' (Moss, 2008b) with voice and agency, and a redefined identity as professional, transformed women practitioners as shown in the pen portrait in Figure 9.1.

The Foundation Degree Graduate

A Transformed Woman Practitioner

A REFLECTIVE PROFESSIONAL PRACTITIONER

o   **She has a reflective self–identity.**
o   **She is confident.**
o   **She has achieved new employment opportunities.**
o   **She has a career.**
o   **She is a lifelong learner.**
o   **She identifies herself as a professional.**
o   **She is an empowered woman – with a voice.**

The Foundation Degree has made me into a professional.

**My confidence allows me
not only to have a voice but to make sure it is heard.**

Figure 9.1   Pen Portrait: a transformed woman practitioner

Work-based reflective learning within higher educational contexts had transformed the FD women graduates personally and professionally, regarding themselves with a new professional identity. This graduate reflects upon her learning journey through her FD studies:

Reflective practitioner's voice

The foundation degree helped me as a mature student getting back to study in a university and getting on the road to study. At the first lecture, I thought what am I doing? But over the three years, I've learnt so much. Before I tended to do things out of habit, I now think a bit more deeply and critically. Is this the right way? What is the right way? Why have we to do this? I can now speak up and question theorists. It's been an amazing journey.

Professional identity and self-perception emerge from personal and professional knowledge, the environment in which teachers and practitioners work, in a school, nursery, early years setting, children's centre, children's services, and personal narratives (Gomez et al., 2000). How did the FD graduates reach the destination of becoming and feeling professional? The graduates' journeys through higher educational learning and the impact this had upon their personal and professional learning, vocational and career progression were explored. A feminist research methodology using a variety of qualitative modes of creative and diverse data collection methods, both experimental and text orientated (Olesen, 2005), enabled the women to story their learning journey autobiographically, allowing their voices to be heard and listened to (Kitzinger, 2007) through lived experience (Clough and Corbett, 2000) validating the women's experience. The telling of narratives provided a retrospective look at key people, and the events that influenced the women's decisions and underlying motives (Court et al., 2009) through their higher educational learning journey.

Five graduates who had significantly vocationally progressed through the FD were invited to take part in a 'reflective learning workshop'. A range of art and collage materials were provided, they were asked as individuals to visually represent their journey through their FD studies using these materials, identifying any key influences and events. Their images were used as a basis for each graduate to write about, further exploring the steps on their learning journey, identifying important events and influences. Bolton (2010) highlights the power of reflective writing in professional learning, through the process of writing each graduate reflectively learnt about their personal and professional learning and celebrated their FD achievement. Each woman's 'reflective learning journey' comprised a visual image and a piece of reflective writing, producing a uniquely personal collection of data, enabling a profound insight into their personal and professional feelings, motives and attitudes (Croft et al., 2009). Data analysis identified emerging themes (Yin, 2003) these were used to understand the women's lived experiences illustrated in their reflective learning journeys. The next part of the chapter presents women's authentic voices, their visual representation and writing showing their personal and professional development through their reflective learning journeys. The narrative telling of their stories; the story structure, its language and characteristics revealed much about the storyteller and her craft of telling and living her life (Ashrat-Pink, 2008). Through narrative, each woman practitioner was able to reflect upon their personal and professional learning and development.

Reflective learning journeys to professionalism

The journey into learning for FD graduates in the case study began with students taking their first small step into higher education, which was daunting for some experienced practitioners who had not studied since leaving school, as for Mel in the first case study, an owner of a private day nursery. Three years and thousands of steps later, she graduated and walked across the stage to receive her certificate, a confident, empowered professional woman (Figure 9.2).

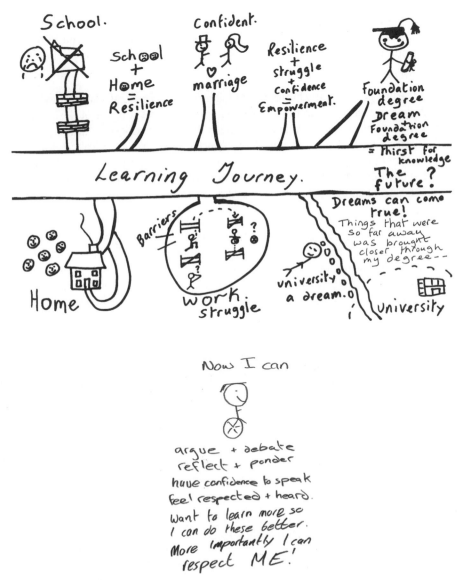

Figure 9.2 Mel's Reflective Learning Journey

Case study: *Mel's Reflective Learning Journey*

The beginning

My true learning journey started from reading a small advertisement about foundation degrees at university. I had all the qualifications I needed to be accepted at university and I could not believe it. I put the advertisement to one side there must be a catch; I thought how could I, merely a nursery nurse, go to university? As I waited patiently to enrol, on several occasions I rang my husband and said I wasn't going to bother, everyone there looked so clever. I was called into the room to complete my enrolment form and the lady who had interviewed me remembered my name. This may seem silly but it made me feel important and like I was in the right place and I had the right to be there.

Graduation

I was the first person in my family to graduate I was so proud, as was my family. I collected my certificate in the fancy dress outfit that was simply not designed to be worn with crutches. As I walked across the stage and looked at the people that had made it possible, I felt proud and empowered as I climbed down at the other side of the stage, glad that I had not lost my cap or fallen down. I felt as though there was nothing I could not do if I put my mind to it. I was still me but now I had a voice that I was confident enough to share with anyone.

Professional identity

I soon realized that the profession I had fought so hard to get into was not actually viewed as a profession. Having qualified in this area as an NVQ 3, people around were devaluing this qualification; I felt as though my profession was viewed as a job anyone could do. Working in an all female environment in a job that was seen as women's work made me realize that whatever I did I would never be a professional.

I have become an advocate for the foundation degree because it has made me into a professional. I am proud of my profession and my achievements. This confidence allows me not only to have a voice, but to make sure it is heard. I question my knowledge as I reflect, and when I reflect my knowledge grows. I am now a professional and woe betide anyone who questions this.

If I had not done the foundation degree, I would still be in a job that women are expected to be in. Now I am sharing my experiences with students and learning from them as a tutor teaching on the foundation degree. I conclude by asking myself what is a foundation degree? Well to me it is academia encased in practice and confidence.

Continuing my learning journey

My learning journey has not yet been concluded, who knows what my next course will teach me or, merely redirect me.

An update

Mel has now completed her BA (Hons) Early Childhood Studies degree and has gained her EYPS; she is an EYPS Assessor and a Fellow of Higher Education. She now owns and manages three private day nurseries.

There are similar reflections within the next case study. Lisa began her learning journey as a nursery nurse and successfully gained two job promotions while studying and as an FD graduate. Lisa visually represented her travel on her learning journey, which she depicts as a 'yellow brick road' (Figure 9.3). As she progresses along it, she subconsciously drew herself bigger, reflecting her emerging personal and professional confidence.

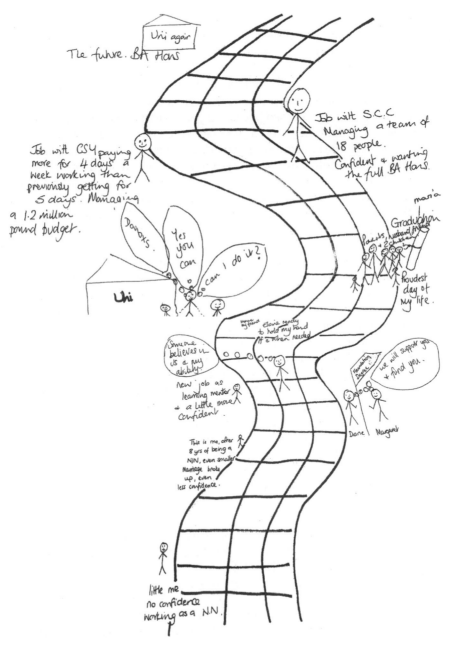

Figure 9.3 Lisa's Reflective Learning Journey

Through her writing, Lisa reflects upon her journey and the influences and impact of her FD award for herself and her family.

 Case study: *Lisa's reflective learning journey*

The beginning

I trained as a nursery nurse when I left school, I 'wasn't clever enough to go on to do A levels or go to university' careers told me, what do you do in your spare time? 'Baby sit as my parents were foster carers', so it's the nursery nurse course for you and off I went to college for two years, qualified and went from one low-paid nannying job to another always working for teachers and head teachers as they appreciated my education values and approach to childcare.

I got pregnant, got married because my dad said I had to at 19, and had two children by the time I was 23 years old. When my youngest was 2 years old I was asked to do some supply work in a nursery as a nursery nurse, I agreed but said only temp work – well one term led to another.

I applied and was successful in gaining the role of a nursery nurse in a newly built 26-place nursery and stayed there for seven years. At first this was the best thing since sliced bread, with no responsibility the nursery teacher I worked with had. After a time, I started to question her values and practice and wanted a bigger say in the set up and care of the children. I did the Advanced Diploma in Childcare and Education (ADCE) when my marriage broke up, basically so that I could have some time for something for myself.

I was successful in gaining a job as a learning mentor at a primary school that was part of an Education Action Zone (EAZ). One day when reading through the literature at lunchtime I came across a flyer about the foundation degree at the university but enrolment was the next day. I phoned the EAZ co-ordinator to ask if there were any places, she said 'yes' and so then I phoned my friend Marie. Off I went to see the head teacher who wasn't at all supportive, but after negotiation and support from the deputy head, it was agreed I could go, as funding was provided by the EAZ. We met at the car park and boarded the bus that took us to the university and enrolled. I expected someone saying to me, go home you are a nursery nurse, or being found out, but we weren't. We went home full of the stories of the university and what life could have been like if we were living there, if only we'd done this earlier in our life.

Starting the course

We went to our first meeting at the university's outreach centre in the local infant school, straight from the day job, with all our hopes and expectations and were greeted by a lecturer from the university. After half an hour I knew that the course wasn't for me, I couldn't understand what he was saying. I went home feeling dejected, I went to the next few lectures always with a heavy heart but knowing that if I pulled out now everyone at school would know, so thought if I failed my first assignment then

I would be pushed off the course – that is, not my fault. I spent so much time on the phone talking to my friend Marie, reaffirming that I wasn't thick as I didn't understand anything and she felt the same way. One night a new lecturer introduced herself, suddenly the context of the course made more sense, she explained everything twice and spoke in English that we understood. At last we handed in our first assignment, and passed, and from then on we were flying! After every assignment my confidence grew and my graduation was the happiest day of my life. My parents came home from Spain for it and my husband and two daughters attended. We hired a minibus with Marie and her family and set off at 6 a.m. so that we weren't late, the graduation didn't start until 9 a.m.!!!!!

Vocational progression

The FD gave me the confidence to apply for a new job as Positive Activities for Young People (PAYP) Manager for the local authority, looking after a £1.2 million budget with double my salary as a nursery nurse. I was appointed on the merit of the FD. In November last year, there was a job advertised for the manager of the Young Offenders Team in the local authority and I was encouraged to apply for it, I didn't because I was a nursery nurse and someone would find me out!!! They didn't appoint and it was re-advertised. I applied and was successful. I now earn £37,000 a year and am in charge of 18 staff. I now know that I need to make the FD into a BA (Hons) and, with the support of my lecturer, my friend Marie and my family, I know I can do this.

Transformational learning

I am the first person to go on to university and my graduation picture hangs proudly in my parents' living room (I carry a small picture in my diary of me and my family at my graduation; when I need confidence, I have a quick look). Not only has this FD degree changed my life but that of my family. It has changed the lives of my sisters, my youngest sister has just qualified as a nurse and my younger sister is on the third year of a social work degree, all following on from the example I set. I feel I have set my daughters a good example and although neither of them want to go to university now, they can do in the future.

I am now treated as a professional in my own right and my opinion is valued, this FD changed the life of my family. I have remarried but I'm not meek and mild anymore, I run my household and I make the decisions that affect my life, and the worst thing in the world now would be going back to being a nursery nurse. How far I have come – as they say from little acorns grow mighty oaks.

An update

Lisa continues to work as a manager of Youth Services in the local authority. She achieved her Bachelor (Hons) in Education Studies degree and is studying for her second degree in Youth Justice. Her daughter has just achieved a first class honours degree. Her friend Marie achieved her Bachelor (Hons) in Education Studies degree and is now an Assistant Service Manager in the local authority.

During the QAA inspection of the FD case study, Lisa said to a QAA inspector 'the FD has been life changing; I wouldn't have my job without it'. Her reflective story shows how life-changing it has been for her, her immediate family and her study partner and friend Marie. The FD case study showed that many new opportunities and doors have been opened through higher education, particularly for women. You may like to reflect upon your own personal and professional learning by illustrating and writing about your learning journey.

〰 Questions for reflection: *My reflective learning journey*

Provide yourself with a table, a large piece of paper and a range of art and collage materials. Reflect upon your personal and professional learning and development through your higher education studies by drawing an image to represent your learning journey through your studies, identifying any key events or significant influences along the way. Then use this visual representation as the basis for reflection, reflectively writing about your journey into learning and the steps along the way. Using a laptop to write will add speed to the reflective process. As you write don't worry about spelling and punctuation; the process of writing provides reflective time and space for you to consider your learning journey. These questions may provide an underpinning framework for reflection:

- How did the key events and significant influences impact upon your personal and professional learning?
- How have your higher educational studies impacted upon your daily work?
- How has your higher educational learning impacted upon your self-awareness, self-belief, personal and professional confidence?
- How has your higher educational learning impacted upon your professional identity?

Transformational influences

From the visual images and reflective writing produced by the graduates in the FD case study, key people, events and influences that were transformational for their personal and professional learning and progression were identified. Telling their life and study narratives created a biographical process for the FD graduates to re-experience and re-examine key people and events from their current perspective

(Court et al., 2009) and enabled them to recognize their personal and professional progression and achievement. Through this reflective process, the following transformational themes emerged: a dream, influential women, empowerment and second educational chance. These themes are now discussed.

A dream

Each graduate had a long-term ambition and goal, described as 'a dream', for academic achievement and their experience as a practitioner to be affirmed, valued and recognized. The FD as a work-based learning higher education award provided a relevant pedagogy for this dream to be realized. The educational aspirations of parents and grandparents who valued education influenced this dream. One graduate described her parents and grandparents as very ambitious for her to achieve, they encouraged her to 'reach my goal and live out my dreams'. Several of the women graduates were from working-class families dominated by strong, ambitious working women who viewed education as a way to opportunity which they had been denied. Court et al. (2009) in their research study of pre-school teachers found the participants' personal history and family background influenced the choice of a professional career. The influence of family members and particularly mothers was pivotal. Similarly, graduates in the FD case study were influenced by women family members and female colleagues they worked with.

Influential women: inspiring and empowering

The women the graduates encountered through their education and employment were very influential in their personal and professional development. For one FD graduate, the women teachers in her primary and secondary education 'were passionate about the education they offered'. She was later influenced by several women teachers who 'inspired her to achieve'.

All graduates had trained as nursery nurses; one graduate valued the all-female learning environment and the leadership of strong women at the college she attended. As the graduates progressed into employment, women leaders, colleagues and lecturers became inspirational role models for their academic and vocational dream to be turned into reality, 'I have continued to be inspired by women leaders'. As in Court et al.'s (2009) study of pre-school teachers, the

FD graduates engaged in meaningful dialogue about values, approaches and perceptions of their practitioner role with women leaders, colleagues and lecturers, gaining aspirations for future roles as teachers, early years leaders or lecturers. Women leaders supported many of the FD graduates during their studies and in their career progression, inspiring and empowering them as early years practitioners. In a community of reflective practitioners, colleagues have a responsibility to support everyone's professional learning, development and career progression. The following questions will help you to reflect upon colleagues who have helped you and on how you have supported others.

 Questions for reflection: *Supporting others*

Think about the people you have worked with, is there a colleague who has inspired, encouraged supported your academic learning and career progression?

- How did they help you?

Is there someone at your work you are mentoring, encouraging and supporting? If so:

- How are you doing this?
- Consider also, why are you doing this?

A second educational chance

Many of the women in the FD case study had been denied access to higher education through educational barriers of academic entry requirements, financial constraints, and family and domestic roles and responsibilities. The underpinning pedagogy of FDs facilitates widening participation and educational access for lifelong learning. The significant contribution of government funding from the Transformation and Graduate Leader Funds (2006–11) enabled a second educational chance for many early years practitioners, particularly women.

 The final chapter reflects upon women practitioner's continuing learning pathways.

Summary

Throughout this chapter, authentic women's voices have been made visible through their higher educational experience of their FD studies. Key influences upon the graduates' academic, vocational and career progression are identified. Through autobiographical storying and reflection upon their learning journey, the women's personal and professional lives were illuminated as they travelled along the transformational pathway to professionalism. The women's reflective learning journeys aim to inspire students and early years practitioners to begin or continue their journey into learning.

Practitioners' lifelong learning journey continues in the concluding chapter.

Further reading

There are some reflective accounts of FD graduates' learning journeys in Chapter 8:
Rawlings, A. *Studying Early Years*. Maidenhead: Open University Press.

This article describes the use of biographical narrative as a research method.
Court, D., Merav, L. and Oran, E. (2009) Pre-school teachers' narratives: a window on personal-professional history, values and beliefs, *International Journal of Early Years Education*, 17(3): 207–217.

10

Continuing Learning Pathways and Future Reflections

Chapter overview

In the previous chapter, graduate practitioners' reflective learning journeys through higher educational learning have been explored. This concluding chapter builds upon that chapter through reflective discussion, considering practitioners' continuing learning pathways in the current early years landscape of change. The contribution of their professional knowledge and research in influencing others and implementing change in provision and practice is examined through case studies. The role of practitioners in encouraging children to engage in reflection is also explored.

This chapter will:
- Consider the place of continuing reflective learning for practitioners within the evolving early years landscape.
- Discuss the impact of practitioners' professional learning and work-based research upon provision and practice.
- Examine children's engagement in reflective learning.

Continuing learning pathways

Continuing to learn throughout a career and demonstrating a commitment to self-improvement or development is a hallmark of being professional and being a member of a profession (Bubb and Earley, 2007). The women graduates in the FD case study on achieving their foundation degree award demonstrated commitment to continuing professional learning and self-improvement, regarding themselves as lifelong learners, as this FD graduate comment shows.

> ### Reflective practitioner's voice
>
> My learning journey has not been concluded, who knows what my next course will teach me.

Abbott and Hevey (2001) proposed a qualification and training ladder for practitioners. A decade on, through broadening of opportunity and government funding, early years practitioners have climbed up the qualifications ladder and progressed vocationally and academically. The FD graduates in the case study, progressed to the final stage of undergraduate degrees and the professional awards of High Level Teaching Assistant and Early Years Professional, some also qualifying as primary teachers. Many practitioners taking these learning opportunities are women, emerging into a unique, confident, knowledgeable, empowered workforce in the front-line of leading policy into practice in early years settings, children's centres, schools and children's services.

The specialized early years knowledge gained through higher educational learning has given practitioners' professional confidence and authority to lead and influence practice. In the national longitudinal research study of graduate leadership (Hadfield et al., 2011) experienced practitioners through their graduate-level leadership training brought together aspects of their professional knowledge base to theoretical frameworks. The training validated their existing knowledge and practice, generally updated or enhanced their knowledge of child development and children as learners, increased their knowledge of the Early Years Foundation Stage curriculum, and developed their experience and practice of working with children under 3 years of age. The integration of existing understandings with new knowledge increased the graduate leaders' level of reflection and criticality within their existing practice and their role in leading the EYFS. Their increased knowledge enabled them to feel more confident in their ability to support, mentor, model practice and appraise staff. They were able to apply their knowledge in leading change in settings, children's centres and service provision, and in leading pedagogy, learning and practice (Hadfield et al., 2011; Hallet, forthcoming).

In influencing change within a school, early years setting or children's centre, the teacher or practitioner influences and leads from a strong foundation of professional knowledge and pedagogy. The professional learning undertaken along the pathway of knowledge comes from a range of key sources of knowledge and events establishing a sound knowledge base and the professional confidence to share knowledge with others, and lead pedagogy, provision and practice. The learning pathway illustrated in Figure 10.1 and described in the following case study demonstrates this. Grace is a reception teacher in a nursery school; she has led pedagogy for literacy learning through play in her nursery school and beyond, sharing practice within local professional

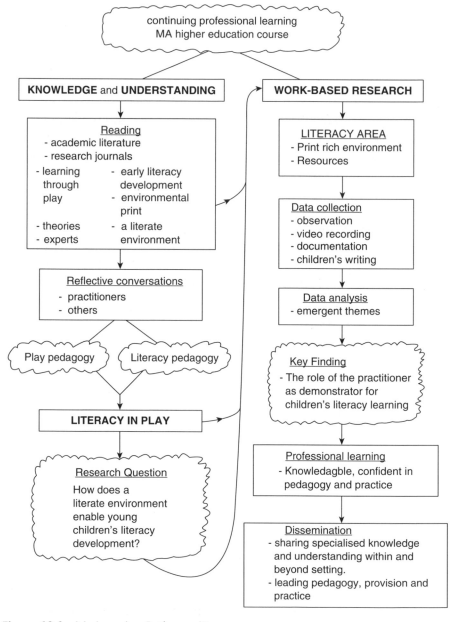

Figure 10.1 My Learning Pathway: literacy area

learning networks. How did she gain the professional knowledge and confidence to do this? The following key sources of knowledge and events gave her specialized professional knowledge, understanding and confidence to influence others, to shape and lead pedagogy, provision and practice.

Key sources of knowledge and events

- Continuing professional development course.
- Reading.
- Reflective conversations.
- Work-based research.

These significant influences in her learning pathway are visually represented in Figure 10.1 and described in the following case study.

 Case Study: *My learning pathway – literacy area*

Grace develops her professional learning as a part-time student studying a postgraduate degree. The course provides her with knowledge and understanding of early years education and includes a work-based research study. Through reading academic literature and research journals, she became familiar with theories and experts writing about play pedagogy and early literacy development. Through conversations with students who were also practitioners in her class, and the lecturer, she reflected upon the theories and ideas from these writers, Bruce, Brock and Ranklin, Hall, Marsh, Whitehead and Wood, gaining knowledge of play and literacy pedagogies for children's learning and developing her own pedagogy of 'literacy in play' for young children's literacy learning.

Grace was particularly influenced by the work of Hall, who highlighted the importance of a literate environment for young children's emergence of literacy (Gillen and Hall, 2003) through meaningful play contexts and the importance of environmental print for children's early literacy learning (Hallet, 2008a). Literacy contexts such as the home corner, a café, a shop, a garage in the outside area provide playful reading and writing opportunities for young children (Brock and Ranklin, 2008). In Wray et al.'s (1989) research they included environmental print in the home corner, making a playful literate environment with resources such as calendars, recipe books, magazines, newspapers, pens and notebooks for children to engage in meaningful literacy actions. Grace's reading and reflections posed the research question, 'How does a literate environment enable young children's literacy learning?' This formed the basis for a small-scale research study, a case study of a literacy area in her Reception classroom for 4-year-old children to playfully learn in.

(Continued)

(Continued)

Grace developed a literate environment in the play area, resourcing it with forms, bus and train timetables, tickets, receipts, toy catalogues, holiday brochures, posters, labels, maps, story books, non-fiction books, comics, magazines, writing materials, postcards, birthday cards, pens, paper, envelopes. A video camera on a tripod recorded children's activity in this literacy area in timed intervals.

She encouraged the literacy area to be an interactive space. At the end of each school day, Grace reflected upon the children's achievements, she wrote letters of celebration to the children, which she left on the writing table in the literacy area.

Dear Steven,

Well done for writing your name all by yourself today.

Love from Miss Taylor

When a child found their letter, s/he replied by writing a letter back to Miss Taylor. This written communication provided meaningful contexts, real purpose and audience for their literacy learning.

Grace viewed the videotape footage of activity in the literacy area and began to examine the data. The children were engaging in various writing activities; however they were not interacting with any of the reading materials. Reflecting upon this, Grace began to understand why. By writing letters to the children she was modelling writing; children viewed her as a writer and responded to her demonstrations by writing back to her and writing to each other. She had not demonstrated any reading behaviours for the children to see. Grace began to interact with the reading materials in the literacy area, sharing pictures and print with the children.

After several demonstrations, Grace video-recorded the children's literacy activities. They were still writing to her and each other, but now they were also interacting with the reading materials, looking and pointing at pictures and print and reading to each other. One sustained literacy activity involved three boys leaning over a map spread out on the floor; they were pointing to symbols and print on the map, identifying the school and local road names. Grace's reflective learning through her research highlighted the importance of the adult's role in a literate environment. It was not sufficient to provide a well-resourced literate environment; the key to its value in children's literacy learning was the resource of literate adults demonstrating literacy practices for children to engage in (Gillen and Hall, 2003).

Through her higher educational study, reading academic literature and research journals, reflective conversations and her own research, Grace was now knowledgebly confident about her pedagogy for literacy learning. With this base of theoretical and practice knowledge, she felt confident to share her specialized knowledge and understanding within her nursery school and beyond in local professional learning networks. She was influencing others by leading pedagogy, provision and practice.

The catalyst for Grace's professional learning was her participation in a higher education course; her research-based postgraduate course enabled her to investigate further her new-found knowledge and understanding, and integrate it within provision and practice.

→ There is a further case study about children's early literacy learning in Chapter 3.

Figure 10.2 and the next case study show how personal interest and experience can inform further professional learning and career progression. Jennie is a teaching assistant in a primary school; in a piece of reflective writing she shares her learning pathway in developing musical pedagogy for children.

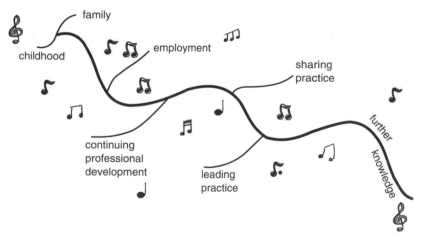

Figure 10.2   My Learning Pathway: musical interaction

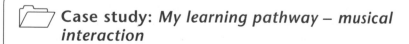

Case study: *My learning pathway – musical interaction*

Introduction

Music has always been part of my life; I wish to share with you my musical learning pathway, highlighting influences and events along the way.

(Continued)

(Continued)

Family and childhood

I've been surrounded by music from an early age. I was made to learn to play the piano and clearly remember daily practice, the weekly lessons and the occasional exams which I passed. I resented this at the time but now I'm so grateful that my parents made me persevere. My family held regular family concerts, all of us having learnt to play a few party pieces . . . fond memories. I enjoyed music at school as noted by the teacher in my school report, she encouraged my interest and this led me to attending a music workshop at summer school.

Employment

Being able to play the piano has helped me get various jobs over the years. I regularly play the piano for assemblies, concerts in school and for the school choir helping children enjoy singing. The choir and the school's drama group joined together and performed the musical show *Oliver!*. I helped with the music and singing, it was hugely successful, very fulfilling for both me and the children.

Continuing professional development and sharing practice

I attended a workshop about using music for children with special educational needs through interactive musical experiences. This inspired me to make my own musical suitcase, an interactive resource, full of puppets, everyday objects and musical instruments. All the items in the suitcase invited children to creatively make music with me and other children.

I was studying part-time for my undergraduate degree; I shared my learning with the lecturer and student practitioners in my class. The lecturer, impressed with my musical suitcase, asked me to run a workshop at the 'Practitioner Conference' in the summer. This seemed quite daunting to me but I thought I'd have a go. I took my suitcase with me and explained how I used it with children with special educational needs and the benefits they gained from musical interaction. I then let the participants interact with the items in the suitcase and creatively make music. The comments on the evaluation forms were very positive, giving me confidence and leading me to want to do more within the field of lecturing. This is where I see my career heading.

I went on a further short course introducing 'Sing Up', the national website for songs within schools, providing me with ideas and inspiration. I'm due to lead a staff meeting on ways of using music throughout the school day. My colleagues are supportive and I'm positively encouraged to be musical within my everyday work with children. Many strands of the EYFS can be achieved through music.

Leading practice

The newly appointed head teacher has recognized my musical interest and expertise and is prepared to allow me to take an active part in leading music throughout the school. At the start of the summer term I will be the music co-ordinator, an exciting if somewhat daunting development.

Further knowledge

I wish to find out more about using music for children's holistic learning, so I'm reading literature and journal articles. I'm carrying out a research study as part of my degree that examines ways to encourage practitioners to use music in all areas of the curriculum.

Conclusion

I hope I have shown, music is close to my heart, my aim is to inspire children, practitioners and teachers, as I have been inspired, to embrace a subject that is traditionally shied away from.

The case studies have provided examples of practitioners continuing their learning; you may like to reflect upon your continuous professional learning pathway.

 Questions for reflection: *Reflecting upon my learning pathway*

Reflect upon your learning pathway; consider an aspect of provision or practice, visually record your learning through drawing or writing. The following questions may help you define your pathway of learning:

- What were the key sources of knowledge you encountered?
- How did these sources help you develop, enhance or gain new knowledge?
- What key events enabled you to learn, modify, change or lead provision and practice?
- How has your newly gained or enhanced knowledge influenced your professional learning and development?
- How has your newly gained or enhanced knowledge influenced your work as a practitioner?

Reflecting with children

As reflection becomes more embedded in early years practitioners' professional behaviour, practitioners are beginning to reflect with children, encouraging them to reflectively think about the environment in which they learn and about their own learning. Through sustained shared thinking in which adults use open-ended questioning to develop children's cognition, imagination and creativity (Siraj-Blatchford, 2007), children's reflective thinking and learning abilities are developed. Encouraging reflective children within the context of children's rights, citizenship and participation enables children's voices to be listened to by significant adults. Hadfield and Waller (2011) found graduate leaders were listening to children more and respecting their views. The United Nations Convention on the Rights of the Child (UNCRC) (1989) and the Children Acts (1989 and 2004) provide a legal framework for listening to children's views, concerns and feelings, hearing the child's voice in the decision-making process (Nutbrown, 2011a). The ability to reflect provides citizens with an ability to contribute to the local community in which they live and to society in general. To encourage children's reflective ability supports their agency and voice.

The Mosaic Approach as a multi-layered research methodology (Clark, 2005; Clark and Moss, 2001) focuses upon children's lived experiences, exploring perceptions of their lives, their interests, priorities and concerns through visual recording and by listening to children. The participatory method allows children to reflect upon lived experience, providing insights into their world. By using cameras, children photograph important aspects of their world; a walking tour around their school or setting with a camera can provide useful insights into children's perspectives of provision, the photographs can provide stimulus for children's reflections.

In the following case study, Amanda, an early years practitioner, undertook a research project involving children in planning and establishing a garden in their pre-school outdoor area, a contrast to the noisier playground. The garden is a place of calm with sensory herbs, shrubs and flowers allowing children the opportunity to sit in a quiet and attractive area. The children call the garden their 'Secret Garden'. Amanda took a group of children on a visual tour of the garden, giving them cameras to photograph important areas of the garden. The photographs were used for children to reflectively talk about, identifying their likes and dislikes by placing them in 'happy face and sad face trays'. Through this reflective activity and discussion, a sense of place within their Secret Garden emerged, as Amanda's writing shows.

📁 Case study: *Reflecting upon a sense of place*

Outdoors has to be somewhere children enjoy being so there is a need to create a sense of 'place' (Bilton, 2010: 143). From the initial design phase and beyond, the children have adopted the name 'The Secret Garden' showing they value the garden as a special place to them, confirming a sense of place in their pre-school. When asked why they have named it thus, the children's responses were immediate and unanimous; 'It's got a secret den', whispered Laura, 'and nobody can see in!' added Betty. Frank told me, 'You can do anything in it . . . and I can be invisible in there!' 'And it's just for kids!' Harry urged. Imogen commented, 'It's got a secret den and the flowers are opening and that's a secret because nobody can see it'.

In creating a sense of place, adults should provide a starting point which gives children focus for their play in areas they can call their own (Bilton, 2010). The den, a wood and bamboo structure with a floor of bark-chippings, has proved to be inspirational, the children using it as a role-play area, transporting resources to enhance their play, a place to quietly sit, to eat in and to have story times in.

The children enjoyed being in the new garden, their visual tour of the area allowed them to reflect upon the area and revealed why it is important to them.

Figure 10.3   Imogen: 'They can't see in!'

(Continued)

(Continued)

Figure 10.4 Frank's 'Imagination door'

Imogen's photograph of the bamboo screens enclosing the garden (Figure 10.3) provoked reflective discussion. Imogen explained 'We can see out, but they (people) can't see in'. Theo disagreed, 'If they get right up close they can look in'. Imogen was determined however, and placed her photograph in the happy face tray; 'I like hiding, I like it because nobody can see me' she said.

Frank photographed the entrance to the den (Figure 10.4) 'I love the den', he said, 'It's got an imagination door . . .'. Asked what he meant by this, Frank explained that each time he went into the den he could be something different: 'Sometimes I can be a dinosaur and sometimes I can be a fighter and I can pretend in it.'

Theo on his visits to the garden likes to rub the leaves of the herbs and then to smell the scent they leave on his hands. During his visual tour, he chose to photograph the herb garden (Figure 10.5). He took the picture, then instinctively held the camera to his face and sniffed it. Theo said with some disappointment, 'It doesn't smell of rosemary . . .'. He then rubbed the rosemary plant with his fingers and then took a photograph of his hand (Figure 10.6). When the photograph of his hand was developed and presented to him, Theo immediately sniffed it, 'It still doesn't smell like rosemary' he complained. He then reflected and took the photograph outside; he rubbed some rosemary leaves against the photograph and sniffed it. 'Now it smells like rosemary!' he enthused.

The involvement of children in designing and participating in the garden gave them a strong sense of place. The use of photographs enabled children to reflect upon why their Secret Garden is a special place for them.

Figure 10.5   The herb garden

Figure 10.6   Theo is disappointed his photograph does not smell of rosemary

As photographers the children became reflective commentators, connecting their physical experiences within the environment to their photographs (Clark and Moss, 2001). Through their photographs children have

(Continued)

(Continued)

embodied their way of seeing, situating themselves within their landscape, not just seeing the environment but reflectively exploring the relationship between themselves, the space, place and objects they encounter (Berger, 1990). Such 'sense of place experiences' can impact upon a child's sense of self, conveying important meaning about who they are and who they might become (Wilson, 1997: 191). By listening to the children through their reflections the practitioners gained insight into their perspectives, informing further development of the garden.

In facilitating children to be reflective, the interactions between adults and children are crucial in encouraging children to reflectively learn from their experiences. The importance of active listening and sensitive intervention is highlighted by Siobhan, an early years practitioner, in her work with young children (Hallet, forthcoming):

Reflective practitioner's voice

For children what reflection encourages is the development of new knowledge, discoveries and new concepts. Through reflection they are able to think about these concepts. If you encourage active learning as well as reflection, then you have two things going on at the same time which is fantastic, in terms of their learning. Whenever I have encouraged children to reflect, I always make time to listen to them. Listening is so important and to value what they say to you, and not just say 'Oh that's very good and well done' but think about taking the questioning further. One example, is when Sayeeda and Lena discovered wet sand wouldn't go through a sieve. So in my questioning, I said 'What are we going to do next? How are we going to problem solve? What are we going to do, to actually see what will go through the sieve?' The girls decided on their own they would change the sand and they would use dry sand. I said 'Wow that is actually an experiment you are carrying out'. So I'm giving them new words as well, which will enable them to reflect upon what they are doing and to discover new things through their learning.

〰 Questions for reflection: *Reflecting with children*

Consider a context in which you encouraged a child or children to reflect upon their learning.

- Consider what you did to encourage children's reflective learning?
- How did the child or children's reflective abilities develop?
- What did the child or children learn?
- What did you learn as a reflective practitioner?

Future reflections

At the time of writing, the early years landscape is evolving and changing through reviews of provision. The Allen, Field, Tickell, Marmot, Munro, Nutbrown reviews (2010–12) significantly reshaped the landscape, highlighting early intervention, child development, children's life chances, health and well-being, safeguarding children, being ready for school, curriculum and early years qualifications. In this evolving space, a new landscape of provision in the 'Foundation Years' from pregnancy to age 5 is emerging. The government's vision for the Foundation Years sets out the importance of intervening early, and of different services working together to provide support for parents and children. The government recognizes the importance of skilled professionals and strong leadership across the sector. A highly skilled, graduate-led workforce is crucial for helping children develop well and prepare for school (DfE, 2011b). The government wants to raise the status of professional practitioners working with young children and ensure they have the skills they need for working with young children, their families, practitioners and agencies in an integrated way. The Nutbrown Review of Early Years Qualifications will consider the content of early years qualifications and how they could be strengthened and develop a career progression pathway for those working in the early years (Nutbrown, 2012).

The future is unknown, however, the professional learning and employment opportunities offered over the past decade have provided a strong and knowledgeable workforce. In this new landscape of reform, it is even more important that practitioners are 'reflective early years practitioners' with the ability to review, consider and critically reflect upon policy and practice through dialogue with others from a strong pedagogical foundation of specialized knowledge, early years principles and practice, so the landscape is transformed into an early years environment that enables children, families and practitioners to flourish.

Summary

The reflective discourse in this chapter, considered practitioners' continuing professional learning through the concept of learning pathways: the contribution of practitioners' professional knowledge in influencing others and change in provision and practice. The role of practitioners in supporting children to engage in reflective

(Continued)

(Continued)

learning has been explored. The case studies provided examples of practitioners' continuous professional learning and children's reflective learning. The chapter concluded by reflecting on the future of the evolving early years landscape and considered the importance of reflective early years practitioners in shaping provision and practice within the landscape of reform.

Further reading

This book provides information about the Mosaic Approach as a research method:
Clark, A. and Moss, P. (2001) *Listening to Young Children: Using the Mosaic Approach.* London: National Children's Bureau.

This book provides information about carrying out work-based research:
Callan, S. and Reed, M. (eds) (2011) *Work-based Research in the Early Years.* London: Sage.

References

Abbott, L. and Hevey, D. (2001) Training to work in the early years: developing the climbing frame, in G. Pugh (ed.), *Contemporary Issues in the Early Years*. London: Paul Chapman Publishing. pp. 179–81.

Adams, K. (2008) What's in a name? Seeking professional status through degree studies within the Scottish early years context, Special Issue, *Professionalism in Early Childhood Education and Care: European Early Childhood Education Research Journal*, 16(2): 242–54.

Aldridge, M. and Evetts, J. (2003) Rethinking the concept of professionalism: the case of journalism, *British Journal of Sociology*, 54: 547–64.

Allen, G. (2011) *Early Intervention: The Next Steps*, London: Her Majesty's Government.

Allix, N. (2011) Knowledge and workplace learning, in M. Malloch, L. Cairns, K. Evans and B.N. O'Conner (eds), *The Sage Handbook of Workplace Learning*. London: Sage. pp.130–48.

Anning, A. and Edwards, A. (2003) The inquiring professional, in A. Anning and A. Edwards, *Promoting Children's Learning from Birth to Five*. Buckingham: Open University Press. pp. 35–58.

Appleby, K. (2010) Reflective thinking: reflective practice, in M. Reed and N. Canning (eds.) *Reflective Practice in the Early Years*. London: Sage. pp. 7–23.

Ashrat-Pink, I. (2008) The transition from student to novice teacher in a narrative environment (in Hebrew). Ph D dissertation. Haifa University.

Bass, B.M. (1985) in H.R. Diaz-Saenz, Transformational leadership, in A. Bryman, D. Collinson, D. Grint, B. Jackson and M. Uhl-Bien (eds), *The Sage Handbook of Leadership*. London: Sage. pp. 299–310.

Beaney, P. (2004) Founded on work? Work-based learning and foundation degrees, *Forward: Foundation Degree Forward Journal* no. 2: 8–10.

Beaney, P. (2006) *Researching Foundation Degrees: Linking Research and Practice*. Lichfield: Foundation Degree Forward.

Bennis, W. and Nanus, B. (1997) Leaders: Strategies for Taking Charge. Cambridge, MA: *Harvard Business Review Press*. p.4.

Berger, J. (1990) *Ways of Seeing*. London: BBC and Penguin Books.

Biggs, J. (1999) *Teaching for Quality Learning at University*. Buckingham: Open University Press.

Bilton, H. (2010) *Outdoor Learning in the Early Years*, 3rd edn. Abingdon: Routledge.

Bolam, R. (1993) Recent development and emerging issues, in *The Continuing Professional Development of Teachers*, 2nd edn. London: General Teaching Council.

Bolton, G. (2005) *Reflective Practice: Writing and Professional Development*. 2nd edn. London: Sage.

Bolton, G. (2010) *Reflective Practice: Writing and Professional Development*. 3rd edn. London: Sage.

Boud, D. and Solomon, N. (2003) Researching Workplace Learning in Australia, in M. Malloch, L. Cairns, K. Evans, and B.N. O'Conner (eds), *The Sage Handbook of Workplace Learning*. London: Sage. pp. 210–223.

Bowlby, J. (1988) *A Secure Base: Clinical Applications of Attachment Theory*. Oxford: Routledge.

Boyd, E. and Fales, A. (1983) Reflective Learning: Key to learning from experience. *Journal of Humanistic Psychology*, 23(2): 99–117.

Brock, A. (2011) Perspectives on Professionalism, in A. Brock and C. Ranklin, *Professionalism in the Interdisciplinary Early Years Team*. London: Continuum. pp. 59–76.

Brock, A. and Ranklin, C. (2008) *Communication, Language and Literacy from Birth to Five Years*. London: Sage

Brock, A. and Ranklin, C. (2011) Professionalism in the Interdisciplinary Early Years Team. London: Continuum.

Bronfenbrenner, U. (1979) The ecology of human development, in Brooker, L. *Supporting Transitions in the Early Years*. Maidenhead: Open University Press. p. 5.

Brookfield, S. (1995) *Becoming a Critically Reflective Teacher*. San Francisco, CA: Jossey-Bass.

Browne, N. (2008) Where are the men? A critical discussion of male absence in the early years, in L. Miller and C. Cable (eds) (2011) *Professionalization, Leadership and Management in the Early Years*. London: Sage. pp. 19–32.

Bubb, S. and Earley, B. (2007) *Leading and Managing Continuing Professional Development*, 2nd ed. London: Paul Chapman Publishing.

Burke, P. (2006) Men accessing education: gendered aspirations, *British Research Journal*, 32(5): 719–33.

Cairns, L. and Malloch, M. (2011) Theories of work, place and learning: new directions, in M. Malloch, L. Cairns, K. Evans and B.N. O'Conner (eds), *The Sage Handbook of Workplace Learning*. London: Sage. pp. 3–16.

Calder, P. (2008) Early childhood studies degrees: the development of a graduate profession, in L. Miller and C. Cable (eds), *Professionalism in the Early Years*. London: Hodder and Stoughton.

Callan, S. and Read, M. (eds) (2011) *Work-based Research in the Early Years*. London: Sage.

Cameron, C. (2004) *Building an Integrated Workforce for a Long-Term Vision of Universal Early Education and Care*. Policy Paper. No 3. London: Daycare Trust.

Cameron, C., Moss, P. and Owen, P. (1999) *Men in the Nursery: Gender and Caring Work*. London: Paul Chapman Publishing.

Carli, L. and Eagly, A. (2011) Gender and leadership, in A. Bryman, D. Collinson, D. Grint, B. Jackson and M. Uhl-Bien (eds), *The Sage Handbook of Leadership*. London: Sage. pp. 103–17.

Carrington, B., Francis, B., Hutchings, M., Skelton, C., Read, B. and Hall, I. (2007) Does the gender of the teacher really matter? Seven- to eight-year-olds' accounts of their interactions with their teachers, *Educational Studies* 33(4): 397– 413.

Challis, M. (2006) The assessment of work-based learning: what is the role of employers? *Forward: Foundation Degree Forward Journal*, no. 7: 8–10.

Children's Workforce Development Council (CWDC) (2006) *A Headstart for All: Early Years Professional Status: Candidate Information*. Leeds. CWDC.

Children's Workforce Development Council (CWDC) (2007) *Guidance for the Standards for the award of Early Years Professional Status.* Nottingham: Children's Workforce Development Council.

Children's Workforce Development Council (CWDC) (2008) *Introduction and Information Guide: Early Years Professionals, Creating Brighter Futures.* Leeds: Children's Workforce Development Council.

Children's Workforce Development Council (CWDC) (2010a) *The Common Core of Skills and Knowledge.* Leeds: Children's Workforce Development Council.

Children's Workforce Development Council (CWDC) (2010b) *Qualifications Curriculum Framework.* Leeds: Children's Workforce Development Council.

Clark, A. (2004) The mosaic approach and research with young children, in V. Lewis, M. Kellett, C. Robinson, S. Fraser and S. Ding (eds) *The Reality of Research with children and young people.* London: Sage.

Clark, A. (2005) Ways of seeing: using the mosaic to listening to young children's perspectives, in A. Clark, T.A. Kjorholt, and P. Moss (eds), *Beyond Listening: Children's Perspective on Early Childhood Services.* Bristol: Policy Press. pp. 29–40.

Clark, A. and Moss, P. (2001) *Listening to Young Children: Using the Mosaic Approach.* London: National Children's Bureau.

Clough, P. and Corbett, J. (2000) in A. Paige-Smith and A. Craft, 2008 (1st edn.) *Developing Reflective Practice in the Early Years.* Maidenhead: Open University Press.

Cooke, G. and Lawton, K. (2008) *For Love or Money: Pay, Progression and Professionalism in the Early Years Workforce.* London: Institute for Public Policy Research.

Collard, J. and Reynolds, C. (2005) *Leadership Gender and Culture in Education.* Maidenhead: Open University Press.

Colley, H. (2006) Learning to Labour with Feeling: class, gender and emotion in childcare education and training, *Contemporary Issues in Early Childhood*, 7(1): 15–29.

Colloby, J. (2009) *The Validation Process for EYPS.* 2nd edn. Exeter: Learning Matters.

Court, D., Merav, L. and Oran, E. (2009) Pre-school teachers' narratives: a window on personal-professional history, values and beliefs, *International Journal of Early Years Education*, 17(3): 207–17.

Costley, C. (2011) Workplace learning and higher education, in M. Malloch, L. Cairns, K. Evans and B.N. O'Conner (eds), *The Sage Handbook of Workplace Learning.* London: Sage. pp. 395–406.

Costley, C. and Armsby, P. (2007) Work-based learning assessed as a mode of study, *Assessment and Evaluation in Higher Education,* 32(1): 21–33.

Croft et al. (2009) in Court, D., Merav, L. and Oran, E. (2009) Pre-school teachers' narratives: a window on personal-professional history, values and beliefs, *International Journal of Early Years Education,* 17(3): 207–17.

Dahlberg, G., Moss, P. and Pence, A. (2007) *Beyond Quality in Early Childhood Education and Care.* 2nd edn. Abingdon: Routledge.

Dalli, C. and Urban, M. (2008) Editorial, *Journal of the European Early Childhood Research Association,* Special Issue, *Professionalism in Early Childhood Education and Care,* 16(2): 131–3.

Department for Education and Employment (DfEE) (2000) *Working with Teaching Assistants – a Good Practice Guide.* London: DfEE.

Department for Education and Skills (DfES) (2001) *Early Years Sector-Endorsed Foundation Degree: Statement of Requirement.* Nottingham: Department for Education and Skills.

Department for Education and Skills (DfES) (2003) *Raising Standards and Tackling Workload: A National Agreement.* London: Department for Education and Skills.

Department for Education and Skills (DfES) (2004) *Every Child Matters: Summary.* Nottingham: DfES Publications.

Department for Education and Skills (DfES) (2005) *Children's Workforce Strategy.* Nottingham: DfES Publications.

Department for Children, Schools and Families (DCSF) (2007) *Early Years Development Team: Early Years Workforce Reform Discussion Paper: July 19, 2007.* London: Department for Children, Schools and Families.

Department for Children, Schools and Families (DCSF) (2008) *Statutory Framework for the Early Years Foundation Stage.* Nottingham: Department for Children, Schools and Families.

Department for Education (DfE) (2011a) *Evaluation of the Graduate Leader Fund – Final Report.* DFE-RR144. London: Department for Education.

Department for Education (DfE) (2011b) *Supporting Families in the Foundation Years.* London: Department for Education.

Department for Education (DfE) (2011c) *Nutbrown Review of Early Education and Childcare Qualifications: Notes on Context and Key Issues.* London: Department for Education.

Department of Education and Science (DES) (1990) *Starting with Quality: The Rumbold Report.* London: Her Majesty's Stationery Office.

Department of Education and Science (DES) (2002) *Senior Practitioner: New Pathways for Professionals.* Nottingham: Department of Education and Science.

Dewey, J. (1933) *How We Think: A Restatement of the Relation of Reflective Thinking to the Educative Process.* Boston: D.C. Heath.

Diaz-Saenz, H.R. (2011) Transformational leadership, in A. Bryman, D. Collinson, D. Grint, B. Jackson and M. Uhl-Bien (eds), *The Sage Handbook of Leadership.* London: Sage. pp. 299–337.

Draper, L. and Duffy, B. (2010) Working with parents, in C. Cable, L. Miller and G. Goodliff (eds), *Working with Children in the Early Years*, 2nd edn. London: Paul Chapman Publishing. pp. 268–79.

Drummond, M. J. (2000) Perceptions of play in a Steiner kindergarten, in L. Abbott and H. Moylett (eds) *Early Education Transformed.* London: Falmer Press.

Duffy, B. and Marshall, J. (2007) Leadership in multi-agency work, in I. Siraj-Blatchford, K. Clarke and M. Needham (eds), *The Team Around the Child.* Stoke-on-Trent: Trentham Books. pp. 105–20.

Duhn, I. (2011) Towards professionalism/s, in L. Miller and C. Cable (eds), *Professionalization, Leadership and Management in the Early Years.* London: Sage. pp. 133–46.

Edwards, A. (2000) Research and Practice: is there a dialogue? in H. Penn (ed) *Early Childhood Services: Theory, Policy and Practice.* Maidenhead: Open University Press. pp.13–23.

Elfer, P., Goldschmied, E. and Selleck, D.Y. (2012) *Key Persons in the Early Years.* 2nd edn. Abingdon: Routledge.

Elliott, J. (2006) *Using Narrative Research in Social Research.* London: Sage.

Evans, K., Guile, D. and Harris, J. (2011) Rethinking work-based learning: for education professionals and professionals who educate, in M. Malloch, L. Cairns, K. Evans and B.N. O'Conner (eds), *The Sage Handbook of Workplace Learning*. London: Sage. pp.149–61.

Fenech, M. and Sumison, J. (2007) in Miller, L. and Cable, C. *Professionalization, Leadership and Management in the Early Years*. London: Sage. p. 4.

Field, F. (2010) *The Foundation Years*: *Preventing Poor Children Becoming Poor Adults*. London: Her Majesty's Government.

Foley, P. and Rixon, A. (eds) (2008) *Changing Children's Services: Working and Learning Together*. Buckingham: Open University Press.

Fook, J. (2010) Beyond reflective practice: reworking the 'critical' in critical reflection, in H. Bradbury, N. Frost, S. Kilminster and M. Zukas (eds), *Beyond Reflective Practice: New Approach to Professional Lifelong Learning*. Abingdon: Routledge. pp. 37–51.

Foundation Degree Forward (2005) *In Brief: Foundation Degrees: Work-based Learning: Briefings for Learning Providers*. D4113WBLmc0505. Lichfield: Foundation Degree Forward.

Friedman, R. (2007) Professionalism in the Early Years, in M. Wild and H. Mitchell (eds) *Early Childhood Studies: Reflective Reader*. Exeter: Learning Matters. pp 124-129.

Friedson, E. (1994) *Professionalism Reborn: Theory, Prophecy and Policy*. Oxford: Polity Press.

Gillen, J. and Hall, N. (2003) The emergence of early childhod literacy, in N. Hall, J. Larson and J. Marsh (eds), *Handbook of Early Childhood Literacy*. London: Sage. pp. 3–12.

Gomez, M.L., Walker, A.B. and Page, M.L. (2000) Personal experience as a guide to teaching, *Teaching and Teacher Education,* 16(7): 731–47.

Guile, D. (2011) Workplace learning in the knowledge economy: the development of vocational practice and social capital, in M. Malloch, L. Cairns, K. Evans and B.N. O'Conner (eds), *The Sage Handbook of Workplace Learning*. London: Sage. pp. 385–94.

Guile, D. and Lucas, N. (1999) Rethinking initial teacher education and professional development in further education: towards the learning professional, in A. Green and N. Lucas (eds) *FE and Lifelong Learning : Realigning the Sector for the Twenty-first Century*. London: Bedford Way Papers, Institute of Education.

Hadfield, M. and Waller, T. (2011) EYPs a force for good, *Nursery World*, January: 27.

Hadfield, M., Jopling, M., Waller, T. and Emira, M. (2011) *Longitudinal Study of EYPS: Interim Report*. 14 March 2011. Wolverhampton: University of Wolverhampton.

Hager, P. (2011) Theories of workplace learning, in M. Malloch, L. Cairns, K. Evans and B.N. O'Conner (eds), *The Sage Handbook of Workplace Learning*. London: Sage. pp. 17–31.

Hallet, E. (2004) The reflective practitioner, in I. MacLeod-Brudenell (ed.), *Advanced Early Years Care and Education*. Oxford: Heinemann. pp. 33–65.

Hallet, E. (2008a) Signs and symbols: children's engagement with environmental print, in J. Marsh and E. Hallet (eds), *Desirable Literacies*. 2nd edn. London: Sage. pp. 61–80.

Hallet, E. (2008b) The reflective practitioner, in I. MacLeod-Brudenell and J. Kay (eds), *Advanced Early Years*. Harlow. Pearson. pp. 41–67.

Hallet, E. (forthcoming) *Leadership of Learning in Early Years and Practice (The LLEAP project)*. London: Institute of Education, University of London.

Haraway, D. and Smith, D. (1995) Reflective in teacher education – towards definition and implementation, in J.R. Ward and S. S. Cotter, Reflection as a visible outcome for pre-service teachers, *Teaching and Teaching Education*, 20(3): 243–57.

Hargreaves, L. and Hopper, B. (2006) Early years, low status? Early years perceptions of their occupational status, *Early Years: An International Journal of Research and Development*, 26(2): 171–86.

Harris, M. and Chrisholm, C. (2011) Beyond the workplace: learning in the lifeplace, in M. Malloch, L. Cairns, K. Evans and B.N. O'Conner (eds), (2011) *The Sage Handbook of Workplace Learning*. London: Sage. pp. 373–84.

Hatton, N. and Smith, D. (1995) Reflective in teacher education – towards definition and implementation, in J.R. Ward and S.S. McCotter (2004) Reflection as a visible outcome for pre-service teachers, *Teacher and Teacher Education*, 20(3): 243–57.

Heist, P. (2005) *Good Practice in the Marketing of Foundation Degrees: A Research-based Guide for Practitioners*. Lichfield: Foundation Degree Forward.

Holland, P. (2003) *We Don't Play with Guns Here: War, Weapon and Superhero Play in the Early Years*. Maidenhead: Open University Press.

Hutchinson, S. (1992) Could in-service training be used to improve the status of nursery nurses in the education system? *Early Child Development and Care*, 81: 117–22.

Jacobs, R.L. and Park, Y. (2009) A proposed conceptual framework of workplace learning: implications for theory development and research in human resource development, *Human Resource Development Review*, 8(2): 133–222.

Jones, C. (2008) Studying the early years foundation degree: student voices, in L. Miller and C. Cable (eds), *Professionalism in the Early Years*. London: Hodder and Stoughton. pp.109–18.

Jones, C. and Pound, L. (2008) *Leadership and Management in the Early Years*. Maidenhead: Open University Press.

Kagan, S. and Bowman, B. (1997) Leadership in early care and education: issues and challenges, in S. Kagan and B. Bowman (eds) *Leadership in Early Care and Education*. Washington, DC: National Association for the Education of Young Children. pp 3–8.

Kay, J. (2005) *Teaching Assistant's Handbook*. London: Continuum.

Kay, J. (2006) *Managing Behaviour in the Early Years*. London: Continuum.

Kelchtermans, G. (1993) Getting the story, understanding the lives: from career stories to teachers' professional development, *Teacher and Teacher Education*, 9(5/6): 443–56.

Kitzinger, C. (2007) Feminist approaches, in C. Searle, G. Gobo, J.F. Gubrium and D. Silverman, *Qualititive Research Practice*. London: Sage. pp 113–28.

Knight, T., Tennant, R., Dillon, L. and Weddell, E. (2006) *National Centre for Social Research Evaluation of the Early Years Sector-Endorsed Foundation Degree: A Qualitative Study of Students' Views and Experiences*. Research Brief No: RB751, April 2006. London: Department for Education and Science.

Knowles, G. (2009) *Ensuring Every Child Matters*. London: Sage.

Lakes, R.D. (2011) Work and learning: from schools to workplaces, in M. Malloch, L. Cairns, K. Evans and B.N. O'Conner (eds), *The Sage Handbook of Workplace Learning*. London: Sage. pp. 3–16.

Lave, J. and Wenger, E. (1991) *Situated Learning: Legitimate Peripheral Participation*. Cambridge: Cambridge University Press.

Leeson, C. (2007) In praise of reflective practice, in J. Willian, R. Parker-Rees and J. Savage (eds), *Early Childhood Studies*, 2nd edn. Exeter: Learning Matters. pp. 171–81.

Leeson, C. (2010) In praise of reflective practice, in R. Parker-Rees, C. Leeson, J. Willan and J. Savage (eds), *Early Childhood Studies*. (3rd edn.) Exeter: Learning Matters. pp. 179–91.

Lloyd, E. and Hallet, E. (2010) Professionalizing the early childhood workforce in England: work in progress or missed opportunity? *Contemporary Issues in Early Childhood*, 11(1): 75–87.

Longhurst, D. (2006) What makes a foundation degree? Briefing for learning providers, *Forward: Foundation Degree Forward Journal*. no. 2.

Loughran, J. (2002) Effective reflective practice in search of meaning in learning about teaching, *Journal of Teacher Education*, 53(1): 33–43.

Lumsden, E. (2008) Developing the early years workforce: student perceptions of the early years sector-endorsed foundation degree, *Vision into Practice: Making Quality a Reality in the Lives of Young Children, International Conference Proceedings 2007*, Dublin Castle: February 8th-10th, 2007, *Centre for Early Childhood Development and Education*. 115–22.

MacLeod-Brudenell, I. (ed.) (2004) *Advanced Early Years Care and Education For Levels 4 and 5*. Oxford: Heinemann.

MacLeod-Brudenell, I. (2008) Trends and traditions in early years education and care, in I. MacLeod-Brudenell and J. Kay (eds), *Advanced Early Years*. 2nd edn. London: Pearson. pp. 15–40.

MacLeod-Brudenell, I. and Kay, J. (eds) (2008) *Advanced Early Years: for Levels 4 and 5*, 2nd edn. London: Pearson Educational.

Malloch, E., Cairns, L., Evans, K. and O'Conner, B.N. (eds) (2011) *The Sage Book of Workplace Learning*. London: Sage.

Manning-Morton, J. (2006) The personal is professional: professionalism and the birth to threes practitioner, *Contemporary Issues in Early Childhood*, 11(1): 75–88.

Marsh, J. (1999) Teletubby tales: popular culture and media education, in J. Marsh and E. Hallet (eds), *Desirable Literacies*. London: Paul Chapman Publishing. pp. 153–174.

Marsick, V.J. and Watkins, K.E. (1999) *Facilitating Learning Organizations*. London: Gower.

Maynard, T. and Thomas, N. (2004) *An Introduction to Early Childhood Studies*. London: Sage.

McGillvray, G. (2008) Nannies, nursery nurses and early years professionals: constructions of professional identity in the early years workforce, *European Early Childhood Education Research Journal*, Special Issue: *Professionalism in Early Childhood Education and Care*, 16(2): 242–54.

McGregor, D. and Cartwright, L. (eds) (2011) *Developing Reflective Practice: A Guide for Beginning Teachers*. Maidenhead: Open University Press.

McMillan, D.J. (2009) Preparing for educare: student perspectives on early years training in Northern Ireland, *International Journal of Early Years Education,*17(3): 219–35.

Menmuir, J. and Hughes, A. (1998) Developing professionalism in early years staff, *The Journal of Early Years,* 19(1): 9–19.

Miller, L. and Cable, C. (2008a) *Professionalism in the Early Years*. Abingdon: Hodder Education.

Miller, L. and Cable, C. (2008b) in Roberts-Holmes, G. and Brownhill, S. Where are the men? A critical discussion of male absence in the early years, in L. Miller and C. Cable (eds) (2011) *Professionalisation, Leadership and Management in the Early Years*. London: Sage. pp. 119–32.

Miller, L. and Cable, C. (eds) (2011) *Professionalization, Leadership and Management in the Early Years*. London: Sage.

Miller, L., Cable, C. and Devereux, J. (2005) Developing professionalism within a regulatory framework in England: challenges and possibilities, *European Early Childhood Education Research Journal*, 16(2): 255–68.

Moon, J. (1999) *Reflection in Learning and Professional Development*. London: RoutledgeFalmer Press.

Moon, J. (2006) *A Handbook of Reflective and Experimental Learning: Theory and Practice*. London: Routledge Falmer.

Moss, P. (2003) *Beyond Caring: The Case for Reforming the Childcare and Early Years Workforce*. Facing the Future Policy Paper No. 5. London: Daycare Trust.

Moss, P. (2008a) Foreword, in A. Paige-Smith and A. Craft (eds), *Developing Reflective Practice*. London: Open University Press. pp. xii–xiv.

Moss, P. (2008b) The democratic and reflective professional: rethinking and reforming the early years workforce, in L. Miller and C. Cable (eds), *Professionalism in the Early Years*. London: Hodder Education. pp. 121–30.

Moss, P. (2011) Foreword, in A. Paige-Smith and A. Craft, *Developing Reflective Practice in the Early Years,* 2011, 2nd edn. Maidenhead: Open University Press. pp. xiii–xviii.

Moyles, J. (2001) Passion, paradox and professionalism in early years education, *Early Years: An International Journal of Research and Development,* 11(1): 8–19.

Moyles, J. (2006) *Effective Leadership and Management in the Early Years*. Maidenhead: Open University Press.

Munro, E. (2010) *Munro Review of Child Protection: DFE 00548-2010*. London: Department for Education.

Nagy Hesse-Biber, S. and Leavy, P. (2006) *Emergent Methods in Social Education*. London: Sage.

National College for School Leadership (NCSL) (2008) *Realising Leadership: Children's Centre Leaders in Action. The Impact of National Professional Qualification in Integrated Centre Leadership (NPQICL) on Children's Centre Leaders and their Practice*. Nottingham: NCSL.

Nelson, A. (2011) Foreword, in C. Aubrey, *Leading and Managing in the Early Years,* 2nd edn. London: Sage.

Newport, F. (2001) Americans see women as emotional and affectionate, men as more aggressive. Gallup Poll News service. Retrieved from: www.gallup.

com/poll/1978/Americans-see-women-emotional-affectionate-men-more-aggressive.aspx.

Nutbrown, C. (2011a) *Key Concepts in Early Childhood Education and Care*, 2nd edn. London: Sage.

Nutbrown, C. (2011b) Department for Education Letter: Launch of the Early Education and Childcare Qualifications Review, DfE, July.

Nutbrown, C. (2012) *Review of Early Education and Childcare Qualifications: Interim Report*, March 2012. London: Department for Education.

Nutbrown, C. and Page, J. (2008) *Working with Babies and Children from Birth to Three Years*. London: Sage.

O'Keefe, J. and Tait, K. (2004) An examination of the UK early years foundation degree and the evolution of senior practitioners – enhancing work-based practice by engaging in reflective and critical thinking, *The International Journal of Early Years Education*, 12(1): 25–41.

Oberhuemer, P. (2005) Conceptualising the early childhood pedagogue: policy approaches and issues of professionalism, *European Early Childhood Education Research Journal*, 9: 57–72.

Olesen, V. (2005) Early millennial feminist qualitative research: challenges and contours, in N. Denzin and Y. Lincoln, *The Sage Handbook of Qualitative Research*. 3rd edn. London: Sage.

Organisation for Economic Co-operation and Development (OECD) (2006) Starting Strong II: Early Childhood Education and Care. Paris: OECD.

Osgood, J. (2006) Professionalism and perfomativity: the feminist challenge facing early years practitioners, *Early Years: International Journal of Research and Development*, 26(2): 187–99.

Osgood, J. (2009) Childcare workforce reform in England and the 'early years professional': a critical discourse analysis, *Journal of Education Policy*, 24(6): 733–51.

Osgood, J. (2011) Contested constructions of professionalism within the nursery, in L. Miller and C. Cable (eds), *Professionalization, Leadership and Management in the Early Years*. London: Sage. pp. 107–18.

Osterman, K.F. and Kottkamp, R.B. (1993) *Reflective Practice for Educators: Improving Schooling through Professional Development*. Thousand Oaks, CA: Corwin Press.

Owen, S. and Haynes, G. (2008) Training and workforce issues in the early years, in G. Pugh and B. Duffy (eds), *Contemporary Issues in the Early Years*. 5th edn. London: Sage. pp. 195–208.

Paige-Smith, A. and Craft, A. (2011) *Developing Reflective Practice in the Early Years*. 2nd edn. Maidenhead: Open University Press.

Peeters, J. (2007) Including men in early childhood education: insights from the European experience, *New Zealand Research in Early Childhood Education*, 10.

Peeters, J. (2008) *The construction of a new profession: A European perspective on professionalism in ECEC*. Amsterdam: SWP Publications. pp. 15–24.

Peeters, J. and Vandenbroeck, M. (2011) Childcare practitioners and the process of professionalisation, in L. Miller and C. Cable (eds), *Professionalization, Leadership and Management in the Early Years*. London: Sage. pp. 62–76.

Penn, H. (2008) *Understanding Early Childhood: Issues and Controversies*. 2nd edn. Maidenhead: Open University Press.

Plummer, K. (2001) *Documents for Life 2: An Invitation to Critical Humanism*. London: Sage.

Pollard, A., Collins, J., Simco, N., Swaffield, S., Warin, J. and Warwick, P. (2002) *Reflective Teaching: Effective and Evidence Informed Professional Practice*. London: Continuum.

Quality Assurance Agency (QAA) (2002) *Foundation Degree Benchmark (final draft)*. Gloucester: Quality Assurance Agency.

Quality Assurance Agency (QAA) (2004) *Foundation Degree Benchmark*. Gloucester: Quality Assurance Agency.

Rawlings, A. (2008) *Studying Early Years: A Guide to Work-based Learning*. Maidenhead: Open University Press.

Reed, M. (2008) Professional development through reflective practice, in A. Paige-Smith and A. Craft (eds) *Developing Reflective Practice in the Early Years*. Maidenhead: Open University Press.

Reed, M. and Canning, N. (eds) (2010) *Reflective Practice in the Early Years*. London: Sage.

Reynolds, K. (1996) Mothers, in B. Madoc-Jones and J. Coates (eds), *An Introduction to Women's Studies*. Oxford: Blackwell. pp. 38–60.

Rinaldi, C. (2005) *In Dialogue with Reggio Emilia: Listening, Researching and Learning*. London. Routledge.

Roberts-Holmes, G. (2011) *Doing your Early Years Research Project*. 2nd edn. London: Sage.

Roberts-Holmes, G. and Brownhill, S. (2011) Where are the men? A critical discussion of male absence in the early years, in L. Miller and C. Cable (eds), *Professionalisation, Leadership and Management in the Early Years*. pp. 119–32.

Robins, A. (ed.) (2006) *Mentoring in the Early Years*. London: Paul Chapman Publishing.

Rodd, J. (2006) *Leadership in Early Childhood*. 3rd edn. Maidenhead: Open University Press.

Rodd, J. (2011) Building and leading a team, in L. Miller, R. Drury and C. Cable (eds), *Extending Professional Practice in the Early Years*. London: Sage. pp. 263–76.

Ruch, G. (2003) in Parker-Rees, R., Leeson, C., Willan, J. and Savage, J. (eds) (2010) *Early Childhood Studies* (3rd ed). Exeter: Learning Matters p. 185.

Rutter, L. (2006) Supporting reflective practice, practice-based learning and assessment for post qualifying social work, *Reflective Practice*, 7(4): 469–82.

Samuelson, I. and Carlsson, M.A. (2008) 'The Playing Learning child': towards a pedagogy of early childhood, *Scandinavian Journal of Educational Research*, 52(6): 623–41.

Schon, D.A. (1983) *The Reflective Practitioner: How Professionals Think in Action*. New York: Basic Books.

Schon, D.A. (1987) *Educating the Reflective Practitioner*. San Francisco: Jossey Bass.

Schon, D.A. (1995) Knowledge and workplace learning, in M. Malloch, L. Cairns, K. Evans and B.N. O'Conner (eds.) (2011) *The Sage Handbook of Workplace Learning*. London: Sage. pp. 130–48.

Schon, D.A. (2007) *The Reflective Practitioner: How Professionals Think in Action*. Aldershot: Ashgate.

Seale, C., Gobo, G., Gubrium, J.F. and Silverman, D. (2007) *Qualitative Research Practice*. London: Sage.

Simkins T., Maxwell, B. and Aspinwall, K. (2009) Developing the whole-school workforce in England: building cultures of engagement, *Professional Development in Education,* 35(3): 433–50.

Sinclair, A. (2011) Being leaders: identities and identity work in leadership, in A. Bryman, D. Collinson, D. Grint, B. Jackson and M. Uhl-Bien (eds), *The Sage Handbook of Leadership.* London: Sage. pp: 508–18.

Siraj-Blatchford, I. (2007) Creativity, communication and collaboration: the identification of pedagogic progression is sustained shared thinking, *Asian-Pacific Journal of Research in Early Childhood Education,* 1(2): 2–23.

Siraj-Blatchford, I. and Manni, L. (2007) *Effective Leadership in the Early Years Sector: The ELEYS Study.* London: The Institute of Education, University of London.

Siraj-Blatchford, I., Clarke, K. and Needham, M. (eds) (2007) *The Team Around the Child: Multi-agency Working in the Early Years.* Stoke-on-Trent: Trentham Books.

Smith, D. (1992) Sociology from women's experience: a reaffirmation: *Sociological Theory,* 10. 183–92.

Snape, D., Parfrement, J. and Finch, S. (2007*) National Centre for Social Research Evaluation of the Early Years Sector-Endorsed Foundation Degree: Findings from the Final Student Survey.* Research Report No: 838. London: Department for Education and Science.

Soloman, N. and Boud, D. (2011) Researching workplace learning in Australia, in M. Malloch, L. Cairns, K. Evans and B.N. O'Conner (eds), *The Sage Handbook of Workplace Learning.* London: Sage. pp. 210–23.

Sylva, K., Melhuish, E., Sammons, P., Siraj-Blatchford, I. and Taggart, B. (2010) *Early Childhood Matters.* London: Sage.

Taggart, G. (2011) Don't we care? The ethics and emotional labour of early years profsssionalism, *Early Years: An International Journal of Research and Development,* 31(1): 85–95.

Tarrant, J. (2000) What is wrong with Competence? In D. J. McMillan (2009) Preparing for educare: Student perspectives on early years training in Northern Ireland. *International Journal of Early Years Education,* 17(3): 219–35.

Teather, S. (2011) Upskilling the workforce, *Nursery World,* January: 27.

Teaching Development Agency (TDA) (2008) *Continuing Professional Development Guidance (CPD).* London: TDA.

Tickell, C. (2011) *The Early Years: Foundations for Life, Health and Learning.* London: Her Majesty's Government.

Tsang, N. (2007) Reflection as Dialogue. *British Journal of Social Work,* 37(4): 681–94.

Tucker, S. (2004) Youth working: professional identities given, received or contested? in J. Roche, S. Tucker, R. Thomson and R. Flyn (eds) *Youth and Society.* London: Sage.

Urban, M. (2008) in Osgood J. (2009) Childcare workforce reform in England and the 'early years professional': a critical discourse analysis, *Journal of Education Policy,* 246: 733–51.

Van Manen, M. (1977) Linking ways of knowing with ways of being in practice, *Curriculum Inquiry.* (6): 205–28.

Vincent, C. and Braun, A. (2010) And Hairdressers are Quite Seedy . . . the moral worth of childcare training. *Contemporary Issues in Early Childhood,* 11(2): 203–13.

Waterland, L. (1988) *Read With Me*. Stroud. Thimble Press.

Wenger, E. (1998) *Communities of Practice, Learning, Meaning, Identity*. New York: Cambridge University Press.

Whalley, M.E. (2008) *Leading Practice in Early Years Settings*. Exeter: Learning Matters.

Whalley, M.E. (2011) Leading and managing in the early years, in L. Miller and C. Cable (eds). *Professionalization, Leadership and Management in the Early Years*. London: Sage. pp 13–28.

Williams, J.E. and Best, D.L. (1990) *Measuring Sex Stereotypes: A Multinational Study*. Newbury Park, CA: Sage.

Wilson, R. (1997) A sense of place, *Journal of Early Childhood Education*, 24(3): 191–4.

Wray, D., Bloom, W. and Hall, N. (1989) *Literacy in Action*. London: The Falmer Press.

Wright, H. (2011) *Women Studying Childcare*. Stoke-on-Trent: Trentham Books.

Yin, R.K. (2003) *Case Study Research Design and Methods*. London: Sage.

Index

Added to a page number 'f' denotes a figure.